If The Way Be Made Clear

Janet SHANNON

outskirts press

If The Way Be Made Clear
All Rights Reserved.
Copyright © 2019 Janet Shannon
v1.0

The opinions expressed in this manuscript are solely the opinions of the author and do not represent the opinions or thoughts of the publisher. The author has represented and warranted full ownership and/or legal right to publish all the materials in this book.

This book may not be reproduced, transmitted, or stored in whole or in part by any means, including graphic, electronic, or mechanical without the express written consent of the publisher except in the case of brief quotations embodied in critical articles and reviews.

Outskirts Press, Inc.
http://www.outskirtspress.com

ISBN: 978-1-4787-8172-1

Cover Photo © 2019 gettyimages.com. All rights reserved - used with permission.

Outskirts Press and the "OP" logo are trademarks belonging to Outskirts Press, Inc.

PRINTED IN THE UNITED STATES OF AMERICA

Table of Contents

Foreword	i
Childhood Images of God	1
Dad	7
Beach's Bike Shop	8
My Basement	11
Mother	14
Fran	16
The Ocean	19
Uniondale	21
Bruce Tinker and Hell	29
Youth Experiences	32
Faith, Feeling, Doubt, and Courage	39
Shifting Stones	47
Princeton, Mountain Experience, and First Ministries	48
A Cup of Cold Water	51
More Travels	54
Director of Christian Education	55
Road Trip West: Flat Land and the Grand Canyon	56
Jim	58
Florida Visit	61

A Wedding, A Goodbye, and Some Coddled Eggs	62
The Crisis	68
My Moses Prayer	72
The House	74
Threshold	76
Don	80
Stepmother Initiation	84
Jane	88
Hardship and Help	91
Blind Creek	96
On Forgiveness	101
Dad's Death	104
If the Way Be Made Clear	108
Fried Chicken	111
Navy Wife	114
Joy Ride	117
A Strange Request	119
A Pitcher of Cold Water	121
Sue's Kitchen	123
Working It Out	125
Leaving Briarwood	128
New Life	130
Philadelphia	134
Kristin and Tom	139
We're in Michigan	143
Unexpected Adventures	145
Minnesota Move	147
Landscape	151
The Celtic Experience	153
Return	155
A Light in the Fog	157
Mother's Death	162
Fran, Again	164

The Grand Canyon Seen Anew and the Desert Appreciated	165
Second Honeymoon	167
Where They Are Now	170
Epilogue	173

Foreword

THE TITLE OF Janet Shannon's memoir comes from the words that close a meeting of the Session, the governing body of a Presbyterian congregation. The Clerk of Session intones, "These actions will take place," and the other members join in with "if the way be made clear."

By using those last six words to encompass her story of spiritual growth, Shannon gives them new resonance, stretching them to suggest questions and possibilities for herself and her readers. What is "the way"? What does it mean for the way to be "made clear"? If the way is not made clear, then what? Do we reverse course, give up?

Even as a young child, Shannon doesn't take "the way" for granted. She's instructed about what God wants from her, but she's not quite sure she buys it. She tests limits. She checks things out for herself. She relishes the moment when the child Jesus breaks the rules.

The stakes get higher as she gets older. The way matters more but is harder to distinguish. How can she know for sure God is real, God is with her?

When the most significant challenge of her adult life arises, she asks God first for a way out, then, eventually, for help following a way she cannot envision.

Ultimately, she doesn't follow a way—she invents one. She figures out how to weave together her roles as ordained minister, stepmother,

mother, and Navy wife. She gets angry, she blunders, she laughs, she asks for help, and she forges a life unlike any she had imagined for herself.

What captivates me is Shannon's honesty and openness as she shares her struggles and uncertainties. She doubts, resists, and ultimately accepts what she has been both burdened and blessed with—a rich spiritual heritage, complex family relationships, a thirst for faith, and a questing spirit.

In this memoir, some questions are answered and some are not. But the way, we learn from Janet Shannon—whether clear or not—can be lived whole-heartedly, gratefully, joyfully, and above all, authentically.

—Christine Sikorski

Childhood Images of God

SATURDAY NIGHTS AT our house were all about preparing for Sunday morning church. After Fran and I had bathed, I would sit on a stool, and Mother would roll my hair in curlers, me cringing with every tug. Dad helped us polish our patent leather shoes with Vaseline. Most importantly, Fran and I filled our church envelopes with some of the money Dad had given us for allowance, printing on the outside the amounts we had decided to designate for missions and for local expenses.

Sometimes, as a special Saturday night treat, Fran and I would be allowed a glass of ginger ale before bed.

On Sunday mornings after breakfast, Mother unrolled my curlers, carefully framing my face in banana curls. Fran and I dressed in frilly dresses, white gloves, and our newly-shined shoes. Mom always said we needed to "give our best to God." I came to understand that included how we looked. Dad warmed up the car as Fran and I made last minute touch-ups.

Union Presbyterian Church, built of stone, with stained glass windows and a bell tower, stood on a corner about two blocks from my parents' bicycle shop. Dad took me up into the tower once. After we had climbed the spidery, spooky ladder, we enjoyed seeing and touching the enormous bell and gazing out at the wonderful view.

We parked and entered the church, Dad staying in the foyer to greet people, and Fran, Mother, and I going off to Sunday school. Mother and I went down the basement, where the Sunday school's Primary Department met. Mother was superintendent of this department, which included grades one through three, and met in a large room. I clambered onto a large metal chair, awaiting my fellow Primaries.

At 9:00, Mother led us in opening exercises. Legs dangling from our too-tall chairs, we learned from Mother the elements of worship and the importance of prayer. We worked on crafts together, most memorably, a papier maché Bible-era village. As class time came to a close, Mother exercised her music teacher skills on us, leading us in the great hymns of the Church as well as children's songs not included in the hymnal.

"We're going to sing 'O, Be Careful,'" she would say. "Everyone stand up and do the motions as we sing together." We would slide clumsily off our chairs, straighten our clothes, point to our eyes, and begin:

"O, be careful, little eyes, what you see.
O, be careful, little eyes, what you see,
for the Father up above is looking down below.
So be careful, little eyes, what you see."

We would continue, pointing to our mouths:
"O, be careful, little tongue, what you say.
O, be careful, little tongue, what you say,
for the Father up above is looking down below.
So be careful, little tongue, what you say."

More verses followed, reminding our hands, feet, ears, etc. to be careful. This song helped me form the idea that God, unquestionably male, sat as a judge up in heaven, constantly monitoring my actions. I decided I had better be good, so God would like and accept me.

"O, Be Careful" is sung to the same tune as "If You're Happy and You Know It," with its verses exhorting the singer to, respectively, "clap your hands," "stomp your feet," "turn around," and "shout amen." We sometimes sang that song, too, but only after "O, Be Careful." I got the message that one is allowed happiness only after paying the price of being good.

I now realize that some of the songs we sang in Sunday school reflected the cautious mood of the times. This was the early 1950s, when the U.S. was recovering from World War II, the Cold War had begun, and Communism was perceived as a huge threat. Air raid drill signals sounded through the hallways of my elementary and junior high schools, prompting students and teachers to "duck and cover." I regularly heard, "There is not a Communist behind every tree. There are three of them." The admonition we repeated in "O, Be Careful" referred to more than how to please God.

We also sang from a hymnal entitled *Primary Hymns for Worship*, which included "When Jesus Was a Little Boy." In this hymn, we learned that as a child, Jesus immediately came when His mother called Him. This portrayal of Jesus as divine in his childhood made me wonder. Was He really perfect as a child?

Well, He probably didn't speak to his mother in the sassy way I spoke to mine. When Mother would instruct me to clean my plate because children in China were hungry, I would retort, "Go ahead and send my food to them."

I liked the story of Jesus in the temple, when His parents have to find Him because He stays behind to talk with the elders. His parents are upset with Him. It gave me some relief to know that Jesus did not always act according to His parents' expectations, and the story nourished my feeling of not always wanting to conform to *my* parents' expectations.

Sometimes we sang,

"Jesus wants me for a sunbeam, to shine for Him each day,
in every way, try to please him, at home, at school, at play.
A sunbeam, a sunbeam, Jesus wants me for a sunbeam.
A sunbeam, a sunbeam, I'll be a sunbeam for Him."

Other times, we sang:

"This little light of mine, I'm going to let it shine.
This little light of mine, I'm going to let it shine.
This little light of mine, I'm going to let it shine,
let it shine, let it shine all the time."

or "Jesus loves me, this I know, for the Bible tells me so.
Little ones to Him belong. They are weak and He is strong.
Yes, Jesus loves me. Yes, Jesus loves me.
Yes, Jesus loves me. The Bible tells me so."

We learned these songs easily, and I felt happy after we sang them, standing in line at the door with the other children antsy to burst out. As I made my way upstairs, and as the week unfolded, though, I didn't think too much about "shining my light."

I found my way to a pew in the middle of the church, where Dad and Fran were already sitting. Mother soon joined us. We rose for the opening hymn, sang, prayed, and listened to readings from the Old and New Testaments. Then, just before the sermon, the ushers dimmed the lights, which I always thought was strange. As a young child in church, I never understood what the minister was saying. He did not give a children's sermon, and my parents emphasized how important it was to say quiet in church—behavior and appearance shared an important position on Sunday morning—so I had no chance to ask questions. My dad often fell asleep, exhausted from working so hard all week in the store.

From the time I was four, Mother and Dad allowed me to take Communion. While other parents felt their children should wait until they were confirmed to partake in this ceremony, my parents felt that a child baptized into the faith, as I had been, was a member of the church, "belonged in the community of faith," and was thus entitled to eat the bread and drink the grape juice that were passed among the pews seven Sundays each year. I would take one of the tiny pieces of bread from a silver tray, then pass the tray to Mother or Dad. Next, one of my parents would hand me a tray with small compartments that each contained a tiny glass of grape juice. I would carefully remove a glass and pass the tray on.

While I didn't connect what was happening to the Last Supper, I knew, even as a small child, that I was part of a community of faith and that this ritual was important to my faith formation. We didn't take Communion every week because some members of the congregation thought that, if we had it too often, the practice would lose its meaning. If it had meaning in the first place, how could we lose it? I wondered.

When I was in the first grade, just learning to read, I would leaf through the hymnal during the sermon, picking out words I knew. I didn't like the lights to be low, because I couldn't see as well. Sometimes, I displayed some exuberance as I turned the pages. My mother would place her hand on the hymnal to signal me to turn the pages more quietly.

My parents not only instructed us about how to behave in church, they modeled for us their deep connections to their faith. I remember each time Fran was sick with pneumonia—which occurred on three different occasions—I saw Mother crying in the kitchen, pleading with God to heal her. God heard her prayers. Fran returned to health every time.

My father read his Bible faithfully every day, becoming well-versed in Biblical content. He told me Bible stories at bedtime with great enthusiasm. My favorites were those that piqued my adventurous spirit. "Tell me the story of Shadrach, Meshach, and Abednego in the fiery furnace, Dad," I would beg, or, "Tell me about Daniel in the lions' den."

When I grew older, Mother came to say prayers with me. We said together the familiar prayer which has circulated through many generations:

"Now I lay me down to sleep.
I pray the Lord my soul to keep.
If I should die before I wake,
I pray the Lord my soul to take."

For years, I said this prayer with Mother, but when I was about ten, I began to worry about the meaning of the words. One night, I told my mother that this might be the night for me to die.

"Why do you think that?" she asked.

"Oh, I just do," I responded.

"But why?"

"Because," I told her, "the prayer says, 'If I die before I wake,' and I have prayed this prayer for so long that I think I'm going to die some night. This is as good a night as any." That nightly prayer, along with "O, Be Careful" taught me that both God and the world in which we lived were scary.

Dad

My family consisted of Dad, Mother, my sister, Fran, who was six-and-a-half years older than me, and me. Dad and Mother owned a bicycle store, Beach's Bike Shop, in the town of Endicott, New York, part of the "Triple Cities" of Endicott, Johnson City, and Binghamton. Dad had graduated from Mansfield State Teacher's College with a science major and gone on to Bliss Electrical School in Washington, D.C. to learn how to be an electrician. He always repaired electrical problems at home.

Dad loved cats and dogs. He would hold our cat Beauty on his lap and say, "nice doggy." He instilled in me a love of nature by telling me bedtime stories of his life in the hills of Mansfield, Pennsylvania, where he grew up with eight brothers, a sister, and a mother and father who worked the land. Mountains and hills surrounded his small town. "Dad," I would say, "Tell me the story of how the horse ran away with you," or "Tell me about the time you were picking blackberries, and your great-grandmother scared the wolf away by clapping wooden boards together." As Dad told these stories again and again, his enthusiasm for them never dimming, something good and golden shone through those days of his early life. The land in which he grew up became my land also.

Beach's Bike Shop

Dad started his business selling auto and bicycle parts on Washington Avenue in Endicott. He moved the store to Main Street sometime in the 1930s. As the business grew, he dropped auto parts and concentrated on selling bicycles and bicycle parts and on repairing bikes. Given that he was a bicycle enthusiast and able to fix just about anything, running the shop suited him. I never heard him say that he wished he had had another career.

Dad set out for the shop every morning at 9:00, after Fran and I had already left for school. The shop was a three-block walk, and from the time I can remember, I loved visiting it to see the new bicycles that Dad had ordered. Some of them were kids' bicycles, which he often displayed in the windows. I was amazed that there could be so many bicycles in one place. Kids at my school knew my Dad ran the bike store and often told me when they had purchased a bicycle there. I sometimes saw them come in to get their bikes repaired, too.

Approaching the shop's entrance, centered between two large windows, I would notice new bicycles or ones wildly decorated. As I entered, I'd look over the bicycles lining both walls. Then I'd glance into the bins filled with screws and bicycle parts, which I could open by leaning across their glass tops and pulling their handles.

Soon after Dad opened the store on Main Street, he hired Chester, a middle-aged man with a sunny personality, to work full-time at the shop. I liked Chester a lot because he was very friendly and happy to be part of the store. Plus, he had dark brown hair and brown eyes, like me. Chester would ask me about my school activities and would often tease me about my banana curls—which I didn't like. He knew I liked bicycles and would often ask "Janet, have you noticed the new bicycles in the store window?" "Yes, I especially like the pink one with decorations on it," I might say.

When I was five, Dad taught me how to ride a bike, running behind so he could catch me if I lost my balance. He had taught Fran when she was little, too. Mom never learned. For my first bike, Dad suggested one from among several 20-inch decorated bicycles. Even though he had 16-inch bikes, he never suggested we learn to ride one of them. He probably knew we would outgrow it fast. From the time I could ride, I often toured the town on my own or with a friend.

Dad often hired high school students to work as apprentices. He liked the young people and was always patient in teaching them. Most of the time, he kept his radio tuned to a Christian station, his way of sharing the Gospel with them. Yet I think they may have been more impressed by his patience than by the radio broadcasts.

Besides Chester and the apprentices, Dad, Mom, Fran, and I were the shop's employees. Mother took care of the financial end of the business, doing "the books" in the back office a few hours each day, and sometimes waiting on customers. When Fran was about 13, she began working at the store on weekends during the summer, waiting on customers, fetching and carrying. Because she was an extrovert, she was well-suited to customer service work.

When I was about 13, I also started working at the store, opening bins for customers so they could select items they wished to purchase, then carrying them to the cash register in the middle of the floor to ring them up. I would punch in the prices, ring up the total, then watch the drawer at the bottom of the register spring open, so I could place money in the drawer and count out change. I am grateful that I learned how to make change from my parents when I was young, since many young people today don't have this skill. After I'd waited on a customer, I might wander back to the repair shop to find Dad fixing bicycles or to the office to find him writing out orders for parts in longhand or calling them in by phone.

I was sometimes timid about waiting on customers, so I liked it when Dad asked me to fetch inner tubes and other parts from the basement. I would make my way down the spooky back stairs carefully, my journey growing darker and darker with every step, until I reached the bottom and could switch on the light bulb hanging from the ceiling. As I rounded the corner of the steps, I would see the bathroom stall in front of me. This was a single toilet with a washbowl. (Today it would be called a unisex bathroom.) The bathroom was contained in a wooden frame which I am sure Dad must have built. As I stepped on the elevated floor, it bent slightly. I wondered if someday it would completely collapse, which added to my feeling of adventure. It never did. On the other side of the aisle from the bathroom stood the bin where Dad stored coal in the years before we changed to heating with gas.

I would scan the shelves in the dimly-lit stock room and select the requested item as quickly as possible. Sometimes I had to climb the ladder, already in the stacks, in order to retrieve the needed part.

The other staircase that led to the basement was located at the front of the store, near where the bins were located. I usually took the back stairs, though, because I liked the spooky atmosphere.

My Basement

WHILE THE BASEMENT of the bike shop gave me a spooky sense of adventure, the basement of my childhood home meant something different to me.

Our basement was divided into functional quadrants surrounding the large central furnace pipes. (I never thought the size of the furnace pipes was unusual until my own children visited the house years later and were frightened by how huge they were.)

The quadrant dedicated to washing clothes once held a delightful surprise for me. Early one morning, knowing Beauty was very pregnant and suspecting where she might choose to have her kittens, I ran down the basement as soon as I awoke. I found her curled in the bottom of the laundry basket on top of a layer of clothes pins, four tiny, black-and-white kittens attached to her. I was so excited!

Two of the other quadrants were dedicated to ironing clothes and storing Dad's paint supplies and tools. The last, most important quadrant, was my playroom.

My two neighborhood friends, Janice and Becky, and I liked playing in this cozy space with its undecorated cinder block walls and high small window, because we could set it up however we wished for our various games of pretend. When we played house, baby carriages and cribs were our props. When we played school, we used a blackboard and chalk. In that space, my friends and I were no longer under the rule of the upstairs world which, though loving, was very proscribed.

One time when I was in second grade, my teacher at my real school said to the class, "Someone has taken John's paper, and I need to know who did it." She looked at me and said, "Janet, you have a guilty look on your face. You must be the one." I did not know that I looked guilty and wondered what made her think I was. I had not taken the paper, and nothing I had done previously would have prompted her to come to this conclusion.

"Janet," she said, "you need to stay after school this afternoon, so we can get to the bottom of this." I was devastated. She had no proof except for the look on my face, but I could look guilty even if I had done nothing wrong. I walked home for lunch at noon, and I was so upset that my mother did not send me back after I'd eaten. Instead, she contacted the teacher to find out the details of what had happened.

Days later, down the basement, we acted this out in a different way. "Who took John's paper?" Mrs. Stone (Becky) asked.

"Janet, you have a guilty look on your face, but I know that you would not take someone else's paper."

"Thank you, Mrs. Stone," I said, smiling and nodding.

Sometimes we staged plays and variety shows. I would play the piano on the first floor while my friends sang downstairs. Other times, we made up short skits and performed them. Sometimes we danced. An old blanket served as a curtain for our nickel performances, when we invited our mothers and my grandmother to be part of the audience. We never took our performances out of the basement. They belonged there. The upstairs world was too proper.

Upstairs, I was expected to perform classical music on the piano when my parents entertained company. It seemed to me we had a lot of company. Because I was shy and never wanted to perform for guests, I acted out by playing hard to find when my mother asked for my "recital." It didn't matter too much what I thought or felt about this forced "show"; it would be better to get it over with than to hear mother complain about it for a long time afterwards.

In the basement, when life had not gone well for us or others, my friends and I could play out our revenge on teachers, principals, and sometimes parents. In the basement, we could correct any perceived wrongdoings and make the world right again. In the basement, my friends and I were free from censure, free from pressure, free to become whatever we wanted—or needed—to become.

Mother

My mother, like most moms in the 1940's and 50's was primarily a stay-at-home mom. She cooked our meals and planted flowers beside our white picket fence. She had majored in Music Education and minored in English at Mansfield State Teacher's College, where she and my Dad met. They were married in 1928.

Though Mother never learned to ride a bicycle, she handled the finances for our family business. She was also a deacon and, as such, helped the "unfortunate," as she referred to members of the congregation who were poor or in special need.

Mother gave piano lessons in our home and was a delightful piano player. She was able to play by ear, but never allowed her students, including me, to do so, because she thought it would prevent us from learning to read music. I took piano lessons from her and am still not able to play by ear. I often feel cheated because of that. One of her favorite songs was "The Beer Barrel Polka," even though she never took a drink in her life. "Alexander's Ragtime Band" was another favorite.

Propriety was important to mother and was important in my early learning environment. I was taught to wait to be excused from the dining table and, of course, to say please and thank you when appropriate.

Mom never wore pants or shorts, even to her last days. She felt they were not feminine. She would tell Fran and me, "Men wear pants, but women should wear dresses." I know that she would not approve of my wearing shorts even now.

Mother wanted everyone to be happy and to express only positive emotions. She was uncomfortable when someone was angry, especially at her. "It is a sin to be angry. Jesus wasn't angry when he drove the money changers out of the Temple. He had righteous indignation." Although she sometimes apologized for sharing any negative feelings, she had her share of what she called, "righteous indignation." She would say, "I'm not criticizing," another prohibitive to which she held.

Mother's need for perfection drove her denial of any negative emotions, especially anger. She compulsively related her hurts to our family but never brought them to the persons who hurt her. Rather, she nurtured those hurts. Her behavior made it very difficult for Fran and me to learn healthy ways to express anger.

I often didn't even know when I was angry. I would get pains in my stomach and nobody knew why. Sometimes I missed school because of them, but even at a young age, I discerned some idea of what they were about. My anger had to go somewhere. Mother had her sick headaches, and I had stomach cramps.

Mother was a wonderful cook and baker. Her specialty was apple pie, which she often made to take to people whenever she felt they needed or wanted one, and even sometimes when they didn't. Her apple pies became her trademark. They were absolutely delicious, and we always appreciated it when some of them were left at home for our consumption. I know her secret apple pie recipe and occasionally use it, but somehow the result never tastes quite the same as hers.

Fran

According to my parents, Fran always did the right thing, whether it was display the right attitude or perform the right action. She was much more accepting of what Dad and Mother wanted.

I, on the other hand, did not always do the right thing. Fran once told me Mother was worried about my behaving like a "tomboy," mostly because I liked to climb the tree in the back yard. I never told Mother that I knew about her concern. I just went on doing what I wanted.

Fran and I were very competitive. We fought a lot. A typical fight sounded like this: "I don't know why you get to go out and have a good time with your friends, Fran, while I have to stay home with Mom and Dad. You get to go places I'll probably never get to go."

"You get to do things with Dad that I never did! He takes you to the park all the time."

"Yeah, but you have a lot more friends than I do."

"So, what do you make of that, Jan?"

"Why are you so popular, I wonder?"

"People just like me better than they like you."

"Are you sure about that? I have all my friends that I play with every day."

"Yeah? That's only three people"

"I have boys, too, that I play games with."

"Jan, you can't get around it. I'm *much* more popular than you."

Fran would go off skating, to the movies, and socializing with her friends, while I wasn't even allowed to walk alone to visit nearby friends. My jealousy was a bit silly, as I was not much of an extrovert. But that didn't stop me from complaining.

I complained to my mother about many things concerning Fran—and I complained a lot.

"Mo-om, why does Fran get new clothes, when I only get hand-me-downs? It's not fair! Then she struts about asking me if I like her new clothes—which she is doing right now."

"You should be thankful that you have a big sister whom you can receive clothes from."

"Well, I'm not!"

Fran's very personality used to bug me. I was irritated by the way she demanded attention from Mom and Dad, always wanting to involve them in whatever she was facing, be it trigonometry or some larger concern. I, on the other hand, was happy to study alone and didn't want my parents to get too involved in my life.

"When you are older you can have more privileges," Mother often told me.

"I can't wait until I am older! And how come you are always on Fran's side and never on mine?"

"It may seem that way to you now, but I am really trying to treat you both fairly."

"What do you call fair?"

"Just cool down a bit, Janet."

"That's what you always say. I'm *not* going to cool down!"

Mother would sometimes get so fed up with Fran and me (mostly me), she would tell us she could "just fly." I was sassy enough to say, "Go ahead and do it."

Fran and I shared some peaceful times, too, such as when our family vacationed at the shore. And we managed to work peacefully together when we did our chores, probably because we both wanted to get through them as quickly as possible. We dusted, took out the trash, and sometimes ran the vacuum cleaner.

Fran and I also liked to play Fox and Geese with friends in the back yard. The fox would chase after the geese and try to tag them or bring them down. Then the two sides would switch.

Maybe our ups and downs were normal. But I certainly didn't like being compared to my sister!

The Ocean

Every summer, the four of us would travel to one of the Jersey beaches, such as Ocean Grove, Wildwood, or Grove City. I would help as much as I could to pack the car. I was so excited. As we got closer to the sea and I could smell the heavy salt water, I was stirred by a sense of wonder. I felt free and joyful. Even as a small child, I felt a sense of coming home.

We stayed in a motel near the water and went daily to the beach. Dad would set up a big, striped beach umbrella for Mother, who would unfold her towel and settle in. Then, Dad, Fran, and I would head for the water.

The three of us frolicked in the waves. Dad would always like to get in the big waves with me, lifting me so they would not completely cover me. We sometimes dug for clams, since Dad knew how to spot them on the shore. We built sand castles. I always collected shells and stones. I still have some of those shells.

I think my favorite place was Wildwood, because Dad and I went on the Wild Mouse, a scary ride in little cars that looked like mice. The tracks of the ride jutted out over the ocean, which was scary enough—but, since I didn't like mice, the look of the cars added to my terror. I only went on that ride once, ever.

I was happy that we could spend a whole week at the shore, away from piano lessons and chores. Fran and I were more relaxed and didn't fight as much. We were consumed by the freedom of the ocean.

.Mom did not like the water and was afraid of it. She had never learned to swim. She sat on the beach under the umbrella, probably praying for our safety, while we had a ball.

Uniondale

On many Saturday evenings throughout the year, after Dad had closed the store, the four of us piled into the car and drove to my Grandma's and Papa's farm in Uniondale, Pennsylvania. Uniondale was surrounded by a part of the Appalachian mountain chain called the Endless Mountains, which shot up much higher than the hills around Endicott.

These grandparents, my mother's parents, lived close to "Pennsylvania Dutch" country. The ancestors of the Pennsylvania Dutch originated in Germany, Switzerland, and Holland, and their name evolved from the "Deutsch" (German) they spoke. Some of them were Amish, some Anabaptists, and others had no particular religious' affiliation. My grandparents were of English descent and devout Presbyterians.

To me, the one-and-a-half hour drive to Uniondale was endless. I would ask over and over from the back seat, "When are we going to get there?" Dad would say, "We're getting closer" or "It's just a little ways now."

Nearly every trip, I would ask, "Dad, can we stop in Susquehanna for ice cream?" Susquehanna was an old railroad town about halfway to Uniondale, and on the occasions when Dad said yes, we'd drive into the town and pull up outside the ice cream store. Dad, Fran, and I would all pile out and enter the store to pick out our favorite flavors.

I don't remember what anyone's favorite flavor was or whether it was a drugstore with a fountain—all I remember is the ice cream. Mom would step out of the car to stretch her legs, but, always worried about her weight, never ordered any ice cream. Fran was much better at not asking every time if we could stop. Maybe it was because she was older or that she had more patience. Whatever the case, it was another way in which Fran appeared to be "better" than me. I ate my ice cream right away, while the others took their time.

Forty-five minutes later, my hands still sticky, I was excited to round the corner outside of Uniondale, and, as our car ascended the hill, catch sight of the farm's long, winding driveway.

Grandma and Papa came out to meet us. Grandma hugged Mother and us girls. Papa shook Dad's hand. They helped us carry in our bags and any food we'd brought with us. We'd sit down to a supper of meat, mashed potatoes, gravy, and homemade bread. Sometimes for dessert, Grandma would bring out a blackberry pie, baked with berries Dad and I had picked from bushes in the pasture. After helping with the dishes, Fran and I might go outside to the field next to the lawn to play on the plank and rope swing Dad had made for us. I assumed the swing was quite reliable because, surely, anything Dad made would last forever. When it broke once while I was swinging, I was shocked. I ran into the house to tell the adults the bad news. Dad came out to fix it, as I knew he would. I called him "The Fixer," because he fixed everything.

We usually waited until Saturday evening to drive to my grandparents' farm, because Dad worked at the store until closing on Saturday. Church took up half the day on Sunday, which made the weekend feel too short. If Chester tended the store on Saturday, though, we could drive to the farm on Friday evening. That meant Dad and I could have more time to wade in the creek or hike in the pasture. I think these walks evoked for him the times he hiked the hills of his own hometown. Sometimes Fran came with us, but my most vivid Saturday memories on the farm include just Dad and me.

As we walked, Dad would notice wildflowers and call them by

name. We would hike to the creek, then wade out among slippery, often treacherous rocks, picking our way carefully, heading for the huge rock we always aimed for. Dad and I would laugh when I slipped but didn't fall in. The uncertainty of that journey, which always presented the possibility of a sudden plunge into deeper water, challenged me and lured me back to the creek. I learned about the creek from my falls. Its flowing water did not stay the same and its differences between one visit and the next were not always obvious. A large rainfall could mean I might be submerged up to my chest when I fell. Even if the large rock was not close to where I fell, its presence encouraged me. Once I reached it, I could decide where to go next.

Sometimes Dad and I brought a picnic out to the rock. We would carry a basket filled with peanut butter and jelly sandwiches and perhaps some fruit, vegetables, and potato chips. We would sit on the rock enjoying our lunch and talking about where we wanted to go next on our adventure. When we finished, we might continue to wade or romp through the woods or head to the lumber mill or the dam. At the mill pond, Dad and I would sometimes boldly ride a wooden raft.

Most weekends, Dad, Fran, and I swam in Lewis Lake, where the minister, Mr. Frank, a shirt-tail relation of ours, owned a cottage. Mother stayed on shore, sometimes chatting with relatives.

A few times, when I was seven or eight, I took the train by myself to visit my grandparents. I remember one of the conductors yelling, "Hot cofFEE?," as he walked through the train car. I was a little apprehensive on the first trip, but afterwards had no worries, knowing my grandparents would meet me at the station.

My grandmother, Belle Williams, viewed her local world from her rocker, which sat before the large kitchen window. From there, she could see most of what Papa wryly called "the metropolis of Uniondale"—the street in front of the farmhouse, the Grange Hall with attached post office, two stores, the beautiful creek, and the lake with its dam. Grandma's view of Uniondale encompassed pretty much everything she knew about the world, a small world broadened only by her reading of the weekly Forest City newspaper. Forest City was a larger town, located about 10 miles from Uniondale, past the cemetery where my parents and grandparents were to be buried.

I wondered as I grew older whether some of the superstitions rampant in that part of Pennsylvania may have crept into some of my grandmother's conversations and habits. I know that she would never allow thirteen people to be at her table, because it might bring bad luck, but I never knew her to use the hex sign or the horseshoe which were signs of good luck in the Pennsylvania Dutch culture.

My grandfather, Rennie Williams, was always ready to recite poetry or sing songs. His famous song was "I Did It," which he was happy to perform upon request. The verses told of a woman who regularly made a series of ridiculous requests, and the chorus Papa sang at the end of each verse was equally ridiculous: "I Did It. I Did IT. I Did as I was Bid." We always laughed hard when he sang this song. I only wish I could remember all of the woman's requests. Despite his willingness to sing and recite, Papa was the quiet one of the pair.

When I ate at my grandparents' home, I always wanted to drink my milk from a special glass I referred to as "the blue glass." It was blue outside, white inside, with a wavy pattern inside and out. I have never seen another glass like it, before or since. When I stayed with Grandma and Papa in the summer, I liked to eat my breakfast at the small, white table in the pantry, alone with my blue glass. Fran and I drank a lot of milk, as Mother thought it was good for our bones.

When I was very young, when we went to the farm, I slept in the same room as Mother and Dad. Later, I moved to the third bedroom, which faced the back yard and from which I could see the barn and the chicken coop. Between Mother's and Dad's room and Fran's room was a walk-through closet which Fran and I used as a hiding place in our games of hide-and-seek. Before bed on Saturday nights, we went through the same rituals as we did at home: bath, hair rolling, preparing our offering envelopes. Baths were more fun, though, because Grandma and Papa had an old tub with feet.

On Sunday mornings, Grandma would make us pancakes and bacon, tidy up the kitchen with Mother's help, and then get ready for church. Grandma was always early or right on time to any gathering she attended. She would don her hat, slide in her favorite hat pin, and announce that she'd be waiting for us in the parlor. She always reminded Fran and me to wear underwear without any holes, in case we were ever taken to the hospital. Even as a young child, I doubted that if we were in an accident the emergency personnel would care about our underwear. I hoped they would be more concerned about our welfare.

With my long curls bobbing on the sides of my head and my patent leather shoes sparkling, I climbed into the back seat, and Dad drove us the few miles to small, steepled Uniondale Presbyterian Church. We pulled into the gravel driveway and, if the gravel parking lot was full, parked on the grass. The small church foyer, which housed a bell that could be pulled with a rope, could hold only a few people, so parishioners who arrived early gathered to greet each other cheerfully on the lawn.

When we entered the church, I said hello to the adults and children already there, then walked down the center aisle toward the upper left corner of the sanctuary, where my kindergarten and preschool class met. Other classes occupied the other corners. While two side aisles led to the front of the church, I always opted for the center aisle, which contained the heat register. That register was the largest I had ever seen. It wasn't like the ones at home that were attached to baseboards. I was mesmerized by its size and depth. I stepped on it carefully. My curiosity was seasoned by caution; though I was interested, I was also a little afraid. What would happen if the large, ominous register suddenly gave way and I ended up in the furnace pipes? Not only did the register's size and depth frighten me, but the updraft of air I felt when I walked over it fascinated me. I held down my dress so it wouldn't blow upwards.

Women and girls always wore dresses or skirts to church. Some wore high-heeled shoes that got stuck in the register's holes. I wondered if people who got married in the church got their shoes stuck as they walked down the aisle.

When I arrived at my class, my teacher, Beverly Burns, who was related to most members of the congregation, greeted me, and I sat down in one of the small wooden chairs that surrounded a rectangular table. The table contained a bunch of cardboard animal-shaped cards with holes punched around the edges, clumps of yarn, and a few blunt needles. Mrs. Burns would say, "Pick a card, Janet, and string the yarn through the holes." I would then pull my chair a little distance from the table to join the other children sewing animal cards or playing with the abacus. I diligently completed a bear, lion, or chicken.

"I'm done," I would say.

"Let me see. Oh, that's so good."

How could it ever be otherwise, I wondered, when all I did was pull yarn through holes? Yet, her words reassured me.

Later, Mrs. Burns said, "Okay, children, come to the table for our story." We pulled our chairs back around the table, and she began. Mrs. Burns was not as good a storyteller as my dad. As she told us a Bible story, I half-listened, often looking toward the back of the church to see if the bell ringer was getting ready to signal the end of Sunday school. Before long, I saw the man in the back of the sanctuary stand with the bell and strike it. *Ting. Ting. Ting.* We all started shuffling. Mrs. Burns quickly ended the story and said a short prayer.

As I walked to the pew where Papa, Grandma, Mom, Dad, and Fran were seated, I watched the organist take her seat on the round stool in front of the old pump organ that stood in the right front corner of the sanctuary. As she flipped a switch to turn it on, I heard the airy sound of wind swishing through it. I slid between Mother and Dad.

When Mr. Frank took his seat behind the pulpit, everyone quieted down. He then stood, but his short stature and my short stature conspired to hide most of him from me. He pronounced words to begin the service, and then we sang. Maybe because we sang so many stanzas that the organist grew tired, the organ, which had started out very loud, began to fade. I thought it might be like riding my bicycle while staying in the same spot. I wanted to pump the organ's pedals myself, sure that I could keep the sound steady. Mom let me try to play it once, but my legs were too short. I had to slouch down on my back to reach the pedals, but then I didn't have enough strength to pump. I eyed that organ every Sunday. I couldn't wait until I grew tall enough to play it.

When Mr. Frank preached, his eyes often reddened, and he would start to cry. He could not speak about Jesus dying on the cross without choking up. We all sat quietly and looked at him, while he swallowed and took a breath to continue. Nobody else got upset like this. I didn't understand his sadness.

Grandma always sat next to Mom, her plump body nicely settled and her small, round, black, hat-pinned hat perfectly positioned on her head. As the minister continued, Grandma often bent sideways and whispered to my mother, "Do you think the roast is burning yet?" a question asked during many a church service. Neither Grandma nor Mom ever left to go take care of the roast, and it always tasted good, so I wasn't sure why my grandmother worried about it so much.

After what seemed like forever, the minister left the pulpit to stand by the church door to shake hands with his congregants. Outside the church, I played in the grass with the other children, waiting for the adults to finish their conversations. Concern over the roast meant we wouldn't be there long.

Back at the house, in the huge farm kitchen, Grandma and Mom prepared dinner at the stove they fed with wood or coal. Sometimes I was sent down to the fruit cellar where my grandmother kept canned goods for us to enjoy throughout the year. I would carefully descend the earthen stairway to retrieve a jar of Grandma's green beans, blackberries, or saccharin pickles, one of my favorites. My very favorite was canned peaches, which were always so soft, unlike the ones at the stores.

Gathered around the big, oval-shaped, oak table, we often ate roast beef purchased from the local slaughterhouse, mashed potatoes, and fresh vegetables. My grandmother's favorite vegetable was rutabaga, which I didn't like at all. Sometimes we had chicken, usually one that Dad, Fran, and I had raised from a chick.

We raised many baby chickens in our basement, in a box heated by a light bulb, transporting them to Grandma's and Papa's farm to finish growing and become our chicken dinners. I felt sorry for the chickens, but it seemed normal to raise them for food, just as it was normal for the neighbors and Grandma and Papa to raise cattle for food. Dinner followed so closely after church, it seemed sometimes, especially when some of the church people joined us, as if it were a continuation of church.

We always said grace before eating, Dad sometimes intoning the words on his own, other times, all of us reciting together: "God is good. God is great. And we thank Him for this food. By His hand, we all are fed. Give us, Lord, this daily bread. Amen." Grandma and Mom placed the platters of food on the table, and we passed them to each other.

What happened at Uniondale Presbyterian Church on Sunday mornings never made sense to me when I was a child. Now I realize that it didn't matter whether I had strung yarn, pumped the organ, or seen the minister cry during the sermon. What mattered is that the people in the church cared about each other. They often saw each other during the week at the post office, the general store, or the Grange Hall, where they shared their joys and sorrows, as well as town gossip. They were often hard on each other in conversations held behind each other's backs, but those judgments were expressions of caring.

When trouble came to someone, they helped. When a loved one died, they grieved. When a baby was born, they rejoiced. They remembered birthdays and anniversaries. On Sundays, they came together to worship. Their gatherings reflected the sacramental nature of their community, which was often felt on Sundays, when guests who understood sacrifice, hard work, and sharing, joined us for dinner around Grandma's table.

Bruce Tinker and Hell

Grandma sat before her window and announced, "Bruce Tinker is coming up the street." Bruce, wearing a long, stained coat over a tattered suit, with his hair messed but hardly noticeable under his large hat, literally lived on the other side of the tracks in Uniondale. No doubt he was headed for my grandparents' house. "What do we have to give him this time?" Grandmother asked. She meant, "What food do we have left over that we can send home with him?" Grandma's announcement sent me to the kitchen to wait for Bruce's knock.

Bruce regularly appeared at the back door of my grandparents' house, the door that everyone used, whether family or guests, because it stood closest to the part of the driveway where people parked. As in my parents' house, we never used the front door. This seemed part of the culture in that section of the country. The back door was the open and friendly door.

By the time Bruce knocked, Grandma had joined me in the kitchen. She opened the door with a greeting: "Hello, Bruce. It's nice to see you again. Come in and get warm." (Because of the two stoves, one wood-burning and one electric, the kitchen was always the warmest room in the house.) I said hello, too, as Bruce stepped over the threshold with a couple of clean bowls in his hands.

"How is life for you these days, Bruce?" Grandma asked.

"Not much new these days. Same old stuff. Here are the dishes from last time."

"Oh, thank you," said Grandma. "I hoped you enjoyed the food."

"Of course I did. What comes from your place is always delicious," he replied, smiling.

Bruce handed Grandma the bowls and sat down. "Did you hear about Betsy Jones?" he asked. "I heard by the grapevine that she's in the Carbondale hospital. Had her gall bladder removed."

"Yes. I did hear about that," Grandma replied. Not much got by her. "Have you heard how she is doing?" Grandma asked, turning toward the ice box.

"Haven't heard a thing," Bruce replied.

As Grandma pulled plates and bowls from the ice box and began preparing a plate for Bruce, the two of them continued to make small talk. I watched Grandma arrange a few pieces of fried chicken, several heaping spoonfuls of mashed potatoes, and a slice of blackberry pie, covering the plate with an old, clean dish towel. She sent me downstairs for a small jar of pickles. When everything was ready, Bruce got to his feet, accepting the plate and jar from Grandma's hands while thanking her, and headed out the door.

Other guests often joined us for dinner, but I noticed that Bruce never quite measured up to a complete welcome at the table, even though he often arrived near dinner time. As a child, I took mental notes on this but never mentioned my observation to my parents or grandparents.

Even though his clothing made him appear very poor and a bit quirky, I liked Bruce. But in my young childhood, I found him to be a mysterious character. I did not really understand how he fit into the town. Everyone knew him and appeared to accept him outwardly, though they often talked about him in his absence. My grandparents told of how Bruce and his wife had once actively participated in the Presbyterian Church, but after his wife died, Bruce's appearance changed.

Often Grandma would ask me to take food to Bruce's house. After she'd spooned steak and vegetables into a bowl or arranged pork chops and potatoes on a plate, she would hand me the towel-wrapped dish, and I would apprehensively make my way to Bruce's house, which sat on a dirt road that extended to an unknown destination—a spooky adventure for me. Before I set out, my parents and grandparents always told me, "Be sure you don't go beyond Bruce's house. Don't go in. Just give him the food and come straight back." My imagination ran wild. Why was I not supposed to go past his house? Where did that road go anyway?

When I was about six, I added up what I knew. While the road past Bruce's house got rougher, it didn't present any obvious hazards. But the grown-ups in my family were adamant about my not traveling down it. So, I reasoned, Bruce's road must lead to . . . hell! Why else would my parents and grandparents warn me so ardently?

My curiosity got the best of me, and I decided I would test this premise. The next time I was asked to deliver food to Bruce, instead of returning immediately, I stealthily walked past his house. Would I be snatched away by some ominous character or swallowed up in a black hole? It took a lot of courage for me to do this. Each time I went a little further, and nothing bad ever happened.

Eventually, I asked my Dad where that road went. He said he'd show me. He took me in the car past Bruce's house, and I discovered that the rough road was a short cut to the other side of town, where the churches stood. Nobody used it, because it was in such poor condition. I was disappointed with the truth, which seemed too ordinary. My imagination was much more exciting than reality.

Many years later, I smiled as I realized that my road through hell ended up at church.

Youth Experiences

As I grew older, I continued to know God existed, but God was far away in heaven someplace. I was no longer afraid of God, but neither did I feel close to God. Unfortunately, the confirmation class I joined at age 12 at Union Presbyterian, in Endicott, did little to advance my spiritual life.

The class, led by Reverend Kerr, met in the room behind the sanctuary, where, for six long weeks, the confirmation candidates memorized the first ten questions and answers of the Westminster Catechism. It was tedious; I was bored; and, I had no idea what these sessions had to do with my spiritual formation. Even though I learned the answers, I sat anxiously, hoping Reverend Kerr would not call on me to recite them.

One session, he opened with, "Today, let's talk about the punctuation of the Lord's Prayer." This didactic approach might help me understand my faith intellectually, but it did little for my personal experience. I was not too surprised by my minister's approach, however. I doubt that he had had much experience dealing with adolescents, and he seemed bent on boring us into a life in the church.

After our six-week class, we met with the Session, the ruling body of the church, which consisted of about twelve men and women. On Pastor Kerr's recommendation, we were accepted into the active membership of the church, a confirmation of the baptismal vows taken on our behalf by our parents. (At the time I had been baptized, Presbyterian babies didn't have individual godparents; the congregation as a whole acted as such. Now, godparents are allowed.) Then, we appeared in front of the congregation, where we were publicly accepted as confirmed members.

In contrast to my dull confirmation class, the New York Billy Graham crusade, which I watched on my grandparents' television set, fascinated me. In order to catch the crusade's beginning, my family had to leave home earlier than usual for the weekend drive to my grandparents' farm. Our television network in Endicott did not televise the crusade.

I felt a special tug on my heart with this campaign, as if I had to see it or would miss something special. I helped with the packing, so we could start our trip as soon as possible. My parents also were eager to watch the crusade. Though my mom had been raised Presbyterian at the Uniondale church, my father had been raised Baptist. While we all attended the Presbyterian Church—not known to be evangelical—both my parents were evangelical Christians.

One evening, after Mother, Dad, Fran, Grandma, Papa, and I had watched the crusade together, I understood that my confirmation had not been adequate to make me a disciple of Christ. Very moved by what Reverend Graham had said about each of us needing to make our own decision to follow Jesus, I walked upstairs by myself, knelt beside my bed, and asked Jesus to come into my heart.

A few years later, my family attended the Billy Graham crusade in Philadelphia. As I listened to Reverend Graham say during his sermon that it was important to make a public confession for Jesus, I felt a tug on my heart so intense, I knew I needed to follow through. I walked alone down the stadium steps and stood in front, where I made a public confession of receiving Jesus into my heart. Mom was happy to see me go forward.

After that experience, I became very evangelical and thought that the most important thing a person could do was make a decision to give his or her life to Christ. I started to walk like Billy Graham said I would, with a spring in my step, although this was more of a conscious effort than instinctive. I did not go so far as to evangelize other people, although it occurred to me that I probably should.

My public confession enhanced the experience of my confirmation. My Christianity became real to me. For the first time in my life, rather than just going through the motions of being a Christian, I felt I knew a little of what the Christian faith was about. I felt more alive. My faith meant living the type of life Christ called me to live, and while I didn't quite know what that meant, I was eager to learn.

In some ways, Mom was a good role model for me. She was devoted to her faith and often spent her days in service to others. She made her delectable apple pies and brought them to people she knew to be sick; she visited people in the nursing home; she called on people she knew to be lonely; she helped Dad in the store; she gave piano lessons. But because she buried her negative emotions in activity, she didn't seem to allow herself her full humanity.

She didn't seem to want me to express my full humanity either. Every morning when I was a teenager, as I approached the bottom landing of the steps, she would look at me and say, "This is the day which the Lord has made, Let us rejoice and be glad in it." Any joy I might have had reaching the bottom of the steps was quickly dissipated by mother's insistence on starting the day on the "right note." I'm sure she was trying to dispel some of the sleepiness and grumpiness that was evident when I first woke up, wanting to help me start the day joyfully, but it never worked. After her demanding greeting, my spirits drooped.

However, every day I dutifully ate my breakfast while trying to put on a happy face. It was another example of resorting to, "If you're happy and you know it, clap your hands," even when I wasn't happy. At least Mom didn't request me to sing that song so bright and early in the morning. That would have been dreadful.

In 1959, Fran entered Westminster College in Newcastle, Pennsylvania, majoring in Elementary Education. Once she was out of the house, there was no more competition between us. I was relieved both of the quarreling and any comparisons to Fran, which made me much happier. And, finally, I had a room of my own!

After a year, Fran transferred to Elmira College in Elmira, New York to be near her boyfriend, Dick Truex.

Pastor Hertzog, who replaced Pastor Kerr a year or two after I had been confirmed, became something of a role model for me. His sermons were much more engaging than Pastor Kerr's had been—even as a junior high student, I took notice of them. Around this time, I decided I wanted to pursue some kind of ministry, and I let Pastor Hertzog know. "Are you interested in making some calls on shut-ins in the congregation?" he asked me. "Yes," I responded.

Pastor Hertzog then began facilitating weekend visits between me and various members of the congregation who were unable to get to church. I already had a little experience with this kind of thing, as Mom had occasionally taken me with her to the nursing home to visit someone I knew. My family was completely supportive of my making these visits, and Pastor Hertzog gave me confidence to make them on my own. Of course, Pastor Hertzog reminded me to make sure the people I visited knew my name and why I was visiting them. When I asked him what I should say to these people when conversation stopped, he told me listening was the most important thing. This advice served me well, and I grew to become a very good listener. Pastor Hertzog must have taken his own advice to the extreme, because people sometimes criticized him for not saying anything during his visits.

I always phoned the person ahead of time to set up a day and time to visit. Sometimes, when I arrived, I was offered refreshments. Sometimes, I played a board game with the person I was visiting. Before I left, I always prayed with the person. Everyone seemed happy to see me and always thanked me for coming. They would see me to the door if they were able.

After the visits, I would meet with Pastor Hertzog to discuss what I'd learned and determine if I'd gathered any information he needed to follow up on. His careful instructions helped my confidence grow. I realize now that these visits were demonstrations of Pastor Hertzog's support of my goal and mainly for my benefit.

Summer church camp, which I attended from the time I was 13 until I was 18, offered me some ways to nurture my new commitment to God. Like church and Sunday school, summer church camp was not up for discussion. I was going; otherwise, according to my parents, my spiritual life would be blighted. Hence, every June, I was packed off with my Bible and swimming suit to Camp Sky Lark. I never got excited about going to camp until I knew my church friends were also going, because some of us could then be in the same cabin. My parents or my friends' parents drove us the short distance to the camp, woods, and lake that would be our home for the next week.

Church camp comprised the closest thing to real camping that I ever did. My family didn't have camping equipment, except for a tent, which I slept in once in the backyard. (I didn't make it through the night without running into the house for real cover and comfort!) I enjoyed most of the camp activities, especially swimming and hiking. On the other hand, I could easily give up the creative activities; I owned several lanyards, all products of summer camp "arts and crafts."

The part of camp I most enjoyed and that helped me grow spiritually was "morning watch," a time right after breakfast when we found a place in the woods to read and think about God. As I sat quietly on a log, I could feel God's Presence—much more than I could in church. I delighted in watching a butterfly in flight and hearing birds call. God was in the world!

Throughout the rest of the year, I was active in my church youth group, which met every Sunday night. We would begin the evening with a short worship service, then engage in discussion, and end with a business meeting. We picked officers back then, so I took my turn as president of the group.

We engaged in social activities and went on trips for fun. This was in the era before the idea of going on mission trips to be of service was popular. Our youth trips often were composed of tourist activities such as visiting the White House or New York City's Metropolitan Art Center. The only religious activity we engaged in, other than fellowship, was visiting famous Christian churches, such as Riverside Church in New York City. I think these trips fostered in me a sense that Christianity did not always have to be so serious. We had lots of fun, and that was important at the time, because the Cold War still had an icy grip on the United States. Three Presbyterian ministers emerged out of that group, including me.

The aftereffects of WWII still hovered around us, and, in our limited way, we understood the country's emphasis on "moral" living, getting families back together, and improving society. Rugged individualism became American society's theme, everyone working hard to get ahead. Like the people around me, I valued tradition, and understood that home, school, and church combined to offer America's children a wholesome upbringing.

When I entered high school, I participated in French Club, went to football games to cheer on our team, and was invited to join a sorority for students with grade averages of 90% or better. Rather than date, I spent time with groups of friends of both sexes. Even prom was a group experience. At the time, I felt the best thing to do was be a good student, so I studied hard. One of my teachers gave my classmates and me a list of books we should read before going to college. I wilted when I saw the list, because, although I had heard of many of them, I had read very few. I do remember that I had read *Lord of the Flies* for class, though!

When I started to think about college, Dad laid out some options. "You could stay around the Triple Cities, or you could broaden your perspective on life and chose a college that is not near here." I was looking for a college that offered Christian Education as a major. By offering me this choice, my dad was giving me a wonderful gift: the freedom to choose a college based on what I really wanted, rather than on location. As it happened, very few colleges offered what I wanted. I decided on "Spencer College," a conservative, non-Presbyterian college in western New York State.

I was so excited to graduate, on that summer night in 1963. I remember very little about the ceremony, not even who spoke at the commencement exercises. What I do remember is that, after the ceremonies, Dad supplied my friends and me with bikes, and we rode around Endicott together. We were quite giddy and happy to be finished with high school.

Faith, Feeling, Doubt, and Courage

During the summer after I was graduated from high school, Fran married Dick, and the two of them moved to Vestal, New York, where Fran became a first-grade teacher.

That fall, I entered Spencer College, where I hoped to pursue a course of study that would prepare me to become a Director of Christian Education. Reverend Hertzog, along with my parents and other adults, advised me against majoring in Christian Education, believing my first focus as an undergraduate should be broadening my understanding of the world. I disagreed. Intent on getting my degree in a maximum of four years, I didn't want to waste time taking any courses I didn't have to.

Because of the evangelical predilections I'd gleaned from my family, my home churches, and my Billy Graham experiences, even though I knew the professors and students at Spencer might be more conservative than me, I still thought the college would be a good fit. I enjoyed my freshman year, taking required general liberal arts classes, while getting used to dorm life and living away from home.

My sophomore year was different. While I hadn't paid a great deal of attention to the college's rules and restrictions my first year, I chafed at them during my second. I didn't mind the prohibitions on tobacco and alcohol (my drink of choice remained ginger ale), but the school's position on movies rankled me. According to Spencer's administration, a student attending a movie was playing with temptation. Therefore, none of us could attend a movie without an upperclassman to act as chaperone. I also became concerned at the college's taboo on interracial dating, which became clear when a male African student and a female Caucasian student began a romantic relationship. While neither the student handbook nor any other official pronouncement prohibited such a relationship, the administration stepped in and announced that it was not in accord with the stance of the college. I was disturbed. How could such a taboo be Christian?

My doubts began to grow. I felt that dragons had come to attack me.

Dr. Mercer, Spencer's president, taught us how important it was to start the day in devotions, gleaning truths from Scripture. I tried to do as he said, rising early, but because of my late night studying, I didn't feel edified—only tired and grumpy. I also felt guilty, as if I were not a faithful Christian. When I read Scripture, I found it dry, unpleasant, and difficult to understand. I kept falling asleep during my morning devotions, flunking the school's idea of what a Christian should be and do.

I had been brought up to believe that while the Scriptures are the Word of God and serve as an inspired witness, they are truth as seen through the understanding of the writers. Professor Birdall, who taught my first Bible course and who adhered to the view that the words of the Bible should be taken literally, criticized my interpretation, contending that my point of view bordered on the heretical. I felt confused and condemned.

Precipitated by the school's rigid messages, my focus shifted from my studies to my own angst and disillusionment. I began to doubt my vocation and wondered if I could really be a disciple of Christ. I had read Bonhoeffer and understood discipleship could be hard, but I didn't know a life following Christ would feel so dismal. The joy that my professors and fellow students insisted was a fruit of Christianity eluded me. I thought about transferring schools, but I didn't know where to go or if I would lose credits in the process.

My downward spiral increased to the point that I began doubting God's existence. God wasn't real to me anymore. How could I have these thoughts, I wondered, after my Presbyterian upbringing, my spiritual experiences, and my youth group leadership? As my spiritual torment continued, I realized I needed to confide in someone. I never thought of confiding in anyone at home, not even Pastor Hertzog, though I realize now he would have understood. I certainly did not want to trouble my parents with my doubts. They would have wondered along with me what had happened, and I didn't feel up to talking to them about my spiritual struggles. Instead, I sought out our college chaplain, Pastor Goldstone, who also pastored the Wesleyan Church in town. I had heard him in chapel, and he seemed open and ready to talk. I wasn't sure if he was the right person, but, desperate as I was, I called him to set up an appointment.

On the appointed day, I walked into town, somewhat nervous and uncertain. I didn't know what to expect and felt I was taking a risk that Pastor Goldstone might not listen or be helpful. When I arrived at his office, Pastor Goldstone welcomed me and gestured to a chair across from his desk. I sat down and immediately began to tell him what I was going through. I told him how the college's teachings seemed to be transforming me into an unbeliever. Because he listened so attentively, I felt comfortable telling him about all that had been tormenting me.

"So often," I told him, "I feel I've made some spiritual gain and I'll feel good about it—like when I responded to the call in chapel to come to the altar to be sanctified [which the Wesleyan Church believes is a second spiritual experience]—and then after a few days, I don't feel or act any differently. That makes me wonder if anything significant happened."

"You're mixing up faith and feeling," Pastor Goldstone responded.

"Maybe I am, but I'm not sure at this point how to separate them," I went on. "I thought I was supposed to feel joyful and happy, but I don't. Dr. Mercer always has this huge smile on his face. It annoys me to see him beam like that all the time."

Pastor Goldstone continued to look directly at me. "You're letting your feelings take control of your life, Janet, and you don't need to do that," he said. "Just because you don't feel in control of your feelings doesn't mean you don't have faith or can't have faith. They are two different things. If you allow your feelings to dictate to you about your faith, you are going to be whipped around a lot."

I shifted in my chair and glanced out the window. "I think I'm supposed to portray a triumphant Christian, who has conquered sin in my life. I feel I should be able to show a sense of my redemption and feel happy about myself, just like in that Sunday school song my mother taught us. *If you're happy and you know it, clap your hands.* Nothing in the song told us what to do if we were unhappy. I'm not clapping my hands about anything at this point in my life."

"You don't have to feel happy all the time in order to have faith. God is still there for you, regardless of how you feel at the moment."

Pastor Goldstone's words gave me permission to live out my faith regardless of how I felt. He gave me confidence that my having doubts, struggles, and despair didn't mean God had forsaken me. Perhaps my doubts hearkened back to my childhood sense of God being scary and my worries that I needed to be perfect to be acceptable to God. Pastor Goldstone assured me that I had not been forsaken and that I was capable of being forgiven. I left his office feeling the relief I had felt as a child when leaning about Jesus running off to the Temple without his parents' permission. Pastor Goldstone had told me what I needed to hear.

I continued my conversations with Pastor Goldstone for several weeks. I felt good leaving campus to visit him. He heard my doubt and accompanied me as I walked through it. He told me that I had a lot of faith to be able to doubt so much. I didn't believe him at first, but as I continued to struggle, I came to understand that I had to have some faith in order to have this amount of doubt. He encouraged me to pursue my understanding of the Scriptures and did not criticize me for what I believed and thought about them. I started to come to life again. Whereas before I felt I'd been standing in a burlap sack, its string drawing more and more tightly around my neck, now I felt the string loosening, the sack falling open.

Yet, despite feeling alive myself, I still didn't feel God was alive to me. I longed for a sign that would assure me of God's Presence and acquired great sympathy for the Old Testament Hebrew judge Gideon. When trouble broke out with the Midianites, God said He was with the people of Israel. Gideon responded by saying "If God is with us, why has all this trouble befallen us?" To be assured that God wanted him to battle the Midianites in order to save Israel, Gideon tested God twice. First, he asked God to allow dew to fall overnight only on the fleece he laid out, leaving the ground around it dry. God did this. Second, Gideon asked that God allow the fleece to remain dry overnight, while the ground around it got wet. Once again, God did as Gideon had asked. Finally, Gideon felt assured that he could distinguish God's voice (Judges 6:36-40).

I needed a fleece. I had to have proof from God that God existed. I made a bargain, telling God that if He were real, when I opened my Bible to a passage that puzzled me, I would have some immediate insight as to the meaning of the passage. I knew I was taking a risk. I took my Bible, crawled onto my bed, and opened to a passage that had puzzled me—I no longer recall which one—and started to read. I felt God's Presence speaking to me in a way I never had before. I continued to read, finding that the Presence stayed, enlightening the Scriptures for me. For the first time since I was twelve, after my initial Billy Graham experience, I understood what I was reading and had some idea of what it meant. I was once again assured that God was real and was good and powerful to fulfill my request. God had acknowledged my fleece.

After we had met several times, Pastor Goldstone asked me if I would talk about my experience of doubt and faith in chapel. I hesitated. He had probably discerned that other students had similar struggles and were hesitant to come forward for fear of being criticized. He encouraged me to speak, knowing my story might be helpful to them. After much thought, I agreed. I was scared. While I felt affirmed by Pastor Goldstone, I was afraid of my professors' criticism. Even though I trusted Pastor Goldstone, I worried that I might be being set up for something for which I wasn't prepared.

On the morning I was to speak, I sat nervously in a chair next to Pastor Goldstone. He introduced me, and I approached the podium and began to speak. I told the professors and my fellow students that, because of the college's rigid rules, I had recently gone through a period of extreme doubt. I told them about my fleece and God's amazing response. I made eye contact with individuals in the congregation, and they seemed to listen carefully to my story. After chapel, several students remarked that they appreciated my testimony. Few of my professors spoke to me about it. I wondered why. Maybe they agreed with some of what I had said but were afraid to admit it, or perhaps it confirmed for them that I was heretical after all.

But I was bolstered by Pastor Goldstone's encouragement. He nurtured in me the confidence I had so desperately needed. My belief became more secure. I began to accept that people at the college who didn't agree with me could practice Christianity in whatever way matched their beliefs, and I could do the same. This proved to be of great help to me in my Christian development. I was much more accepting of others' faith journeys, regardless of what they believed.

Throughout my years at Spencer, sometimes alone and sometimes with friends, particularly Carol, I would visit Letchworth State Park, a short drive from campus. As I looked into the canyon in the middle of the park, I saw how large and deep it was. Classmates had likened it to the Grand Canyon, which I had never visited. I couldn't imagine how much larger than Letchworth's canyon it could be. I was aware of the Presence in the wind which blew softly on my face and the birds that chirped happily. Not many birds inhabited the park, but those that did, especially those that sang, relieved some of my angst. Away from the rigidness of the college, I could breathe the air and feel refreshed. Here I often realized the greatness of God in creating such a world, regardless of how it was accomplished. I could connect to God here through the Presence I felt.

Back at the college, I remembered Pastor Hertzog's advice and decided to broaden my studies. I changed my major course and began an augmented history major, which meant I could study the social sciences. I also added minors in French and Secondary Education. The history department was very good, and I could speak with my history and education professors without feeling unduly judged. My mentors back home were supportive of my choices, and I began studying harder and enjoying being a college student again. My World History professor, Dr. Lincoln, was one of the more progressive thinkers on campus, and I felt support from her to have some divergent views on theology.

In my junior year, I began researching seminaries. I rejected out-of-hand the notion of attending Asbury Seminary, the Wesleyan Methodist Seminary in Kentucky where most of Spencer's students went to prepare for the ministry after graduation. I had had enough of Wesleyan conservatism. I also decided against the Presbyterian School of Christian education in Richmond, Virginia. Ultimately, I set my heart on Princeton, whose Christian Education department was very good. I liked the fact that it was close to the Princeton University campus. Although the seminary and university operated as two separate schools, the seminary used some university facilities, such as the library, infirmary, and sports courts.

When it came time to apply, I asked Dr. Lincoln to fill out a recommendation for me. She looked at me warily. "Janet, I hope you have explored other seminaries," she said. Despite her relatively progressive views, I knew she wanted me to apply to a more conservative school—she wasn't *that* progressive!

"But I've chosen Princeton because it offers what I want."

"And what is it you want?" she asked.

"A good Christian Education program which matches my values . . . and where I can explore various philosophies freely."

"You know the school is pretty liberal, don't you?" She locked eyes with me.

"Yes. That's okay."

Dr. Lincoln wasn't satisfied. "Have you considered applying to Asbury Seminary?"

Because my confidence had grown in the last few years, I was able to look directly at her and answer: "I don't think it's the best place for me right now. I want to go to a Presbyterian seminary."

"I see." I could hear the disappointment in her voice. "Yes," she said. "I will fill this out for you."

Shifting Stones

As I matured, my grandparents aged. When they could no longer manage the farm, they sold it. Mom and Dad added a grandparents' addition to the house, which included a bedroom and bathroom, and Grandma and Papa moved in with them. Grandma helped with the cooking, and she and Papa took all their meals with my parents, and me, too, of course, when I was home for vacations. I was always happy to return and be welcomed by my family and our new cats, Sugar and Spice.

I missed my walks through the fields with Dad to look for blackberries and our hikes to the creek. He and I had new adventures, however.

Before I started at Princeton, Dad and I took a trip to England together—a thank-you gift from the Raleigh Bicycle Company to Dad for selling Raleigh bicycles. Mom felt she could not leave her parents to go with Dad on the trip, but I'm not sure she would have gone anyway, because she did not like to travel much. I think she was glad she had an excuse to stay home.

I already was quite close to my father, and this trip drew us closer. I saw more of his personality and learned how compulsive he could be at times.

What surprised me as we walked the streets of England was that people recognized us as being from the States. I knew this when they came up to us and asked, "Are you from the States or Canada?" Did we look that much different, I wondered?

Princeton, Mountain Experience, and First Ministries

In the fall of 1967, at the age of 22, my perspective broadened a little by my trip abroad, I committed to a better understanding of the world and God and entered Princeton Seminary for a two-year course of study in Christian Education. Knowing no other incoming students nor what this leap into a progressive seminary would entail, I was suddenly inserted into a community immersed in racial and political issues. While many of my later colleagues think of Princeton as conservative, after the archconservative Christianity I'd experienced at Spencer, to me it seemed wildly liberal. I plunged into my classes excitedly, expanding my world view through discussions with fellow students, professors, and visiting speakers.

I made some wonderful friends at Princeton. Joyce, my first-year roommate, was a candidate for the ordained ministry and interested in having a church of her own. From her I learned that the ordained ministry was not completely open to women, though after she was graduated, Joyce did find a church to pastor.

I also struck up a friendship with Dolores, an older student who lived in the same off campus housing. We developed a deep friendship which lasts to this day. Dolores had a wonderful sense of humor which would often be manifested in our walks to the other campus. After she finished her training, I continued to join her on weekends in New York City, where she entertained me at the Manhattan Club.

The mood on campus was restless. The United States was in the middle of the Vietnam War, and many students were caught up in anti-war demonstrations. Black militants came to campus to educate us about civil rights issues. I had to confront my own racism, which I realized had been instilled in me, in part, by my beloved father. In this atmosphere of change, women on campus began complaining to administration about being housed several blocks further from the main campus than the men. My inner life mirrored the restlessness around me as I tried to determine what to do with my life. Did I really want to pursue Christian Education?

Princeton's grounds and architecture were beautiful, especially on the university campus. I appreciated the well-manicured grounds and the beautiful walks I took in nature. It was always refreshing to me to hear the birds chirping in the trees and to see the ivy entwining the buildings. In the town, the stores were exclusive—very high-priced. The town was like a storybook, where the real world did not exist.

Between my first and second years at Princeton, during the summer of 1968, I was offered a student internship at Cranberry Lake and Star Lake churches in the Adirondacks. Congregants in the Cranberry Lake Church often boated to services, which were held by the lake—a novelty for me. During that summer, as I learned from Pastor White what it meant to be a pastoral intern, I drew on my lessons from Pastor Hertzog. While in high school I had only visited people in their homes, during that summer, with Pastor White's guidance, I also visited people in hospital. I still was not able to perform any formal religious functions, but as I had in high school, I prayed with everyone I visited.

I also had one opportunity to preach, and while the congregation who heard me was a friendly one, I was nervous. Pastor White probably should have reviewed my sermon with me. I made the mistake of saying that if children wanted to write on the walls of the house, their parents should let them. What made me say this, I'm not sure, but there was quite a reaction from parishioners. Even though they understood my rebellion against stringent rules, they said this was just too lenient. I know now they were right. Perhaps I was reacting to my own strict childhood and youth.

During that summer, I had what I call my Mountain Experience, which dramatically deepened my sense of God's Presence in nature. This experience was a three-month long immersion in the natural setting in which I found myself. I was inspired and enchanted by the folds of the mountain ranges, which looked like verdant green breasts nestled close together. Each evening, after spending all day with people, I would return to my apartment and walk into the mountains to the same spot. As I stood still and listened for the call of the wild, which came over the breeze as a bird called out or I heard some animal of prey call forth, I saw a huge, beautiful sanctuary before me. After giving to people all day, there, each evening, I was put back together.

I felt the Presence of God rustling through the trees as the leaves waved together in the wind. Time was of no consequence. I came alive as the gentle breeze on my cheeks whispered words of hope and encouragement, assuaging my loneliness. The picture is still in my mind even as I write this many years later. I am convinced it will not leave me in this life nor will the stillness and nearness of the Presence I felt there. During that summer in the mountains, I became aware I might someday become an ordained minister.

In the fall of 1968, thinking more seriously about the prospect of future ordination, I renewed my commitment to my studies. At the end of two years at Princeton, I received the Master of Arts degree in Christian Education. My mother, father, and Fran all attended my commencement exercises, Dad with a large smile on his face, something he wore when things were going well. I said some hard goodbyes to friends, but knew we would keep in touch.

A Cup of Cold Water

I REALIZED I needed more experience ministering to people, so I arranged to participate in Clinical Pastoral Education (CPE) immediately after I graduated. In the summer of 1969, I moved to Park Ridge, Illinois, a suburb of Chicago, to undertake CPE while serving as a hospital chaplain at Lutheran General Hospital.

In CPE, small groups of divinity students operate as hospital chaplains, meeting weekly to review their interactions with patients and examine their own beliefs. Given that patients are of various faiths, backgrounds, and temperaments, the chaplains often find their desire to minister bump up against complexities. Clinical Pastoral Education students both challenge and support one another as they navigate their roles. Sometimes, however, I found that what I was called upon to do as a hospital chaplain was not at all complex.

One night, when I was taking my on-call shift, sleeping at the hospital, the phone at my bedside wakened me.

"Hello, Chaplain?"

"Yes, this is Chaplain Shannon."

The voice on the other end was that of a nurse in the emergency room. "We have an elderly man down here named Henry, who came from a local nursing home. He's agitated and we can't decipher the cause. Would you please come down here and talk to him?"

"Sure," I said. "I'll be over as soon as I can." I was surprised by the nature of the call, since a lot of effort was made on the part of CPE administrators to educate the hospital staff about the chaplain's role. This request was outside the norm; usually staff members were able to explain the nature of a patient's problem to the chaplain. As I entered the ER, I gathered more information from the nurse about Henry, including the fact that he was a paraplegic. She then directed me to the back room, where Henry waited in an anxious state.

"Hello, I'm Chaplain Shannon," I said, "and you're Henry. Is that correct?"

He nodded.

"What can I do for you?"

He struggled to talk, and I was unable to understand his words.

"I'm sorry. I didn't hear that," I said.

I bent down to get closer to his face and listened carefully the second time. I could barely hear his words over the noise of the busy emergency room. He said, "I've asked . . . ," then, once again, his words were lost.

I tried again. "I heard you say that you've asked, but I still need to hear the rest of the sentence."

Henry choked out more words, and this time I understood the whole sentence. "I've asked—all day—for a cup of water—and no one has given me one." I looked into his distressed face, then turned to the faucet, jerked a cup from the dispenser, filled it with water, and held it for him as he drank it all.

"Do you want more?" I asked.

Henry nodded. Once again, I filled the cup and gave it to him. Once again, he drank it all.

"More," he said.

A third time, I filled the cup and gave it to Henry. This time, I noticed him slowing down. After he finished his third cupful of water, his body relaxed, his agitated movements stopped, and a look of peace came over his face.

"Thank you," he said.

"You're welcome," I answered.

I stayed and talked with Henry a few minutes before I returned to the desk to give the nurse my report. She thanked me, and I left, recognizing that I had met Christ in this thirsty, agitated man. In this case, finding Christ meant getting down to where living gets tough and people live forgotten, painful lives.

I learned that night that, as Pastor Hertzog taught me, listening is the most important thing. If others won't or can't take time to listen carefully to a vulnerable person, I can. And, sometimes, all I have to offer another person, besides my careful attention, is a cup of cold water.

The "cup of cold water" became a metaphor for my ministry.

More Travels

Dad and I enjoyed two more trips to Europe compliments of the Raleigh Bicycle Company, one to Rome and one to Greece. Most of the hotels we stayed in were quite Americanized, but we attended a toga party in Rome, where we all wore togas provided by Raleigh. Dad and I felt quite conspicuous wearing our togas, which crossed one shoulder and came across the front. Yet, we had a fun dinner and party at the hotel that evening.

In Greece, we visited ancient ruins, including the Parthenon. But I was more affected by the fact that I was traveling through countries the Apostle Paul had visited on his itinerant preaching journeys. In Corinth, I wanted to believe, we walked where Paul had walked.

Meanwhile, my beloved grandmother, who had long suffered from diabetes and other health conditions, died August 9, 1969. I was sad to lose her but convinced she had gone to a better place.

Director of Christian Education

After seminary, I was hired to serve as Director of Christian Education in a church in Ohio. I served there for two years, before the minister was accused of sexual misconduct with a member of the church. I knew I was in the real world then! I decided to seek a position elsewhere.

My next call was to a church in Indiana, where I served children and families full-time. As the church increased in size, my position changed in a way I didn't like: another staff member was hired to serve youth, which made the scope of my position feel too narrow to me. During these years working in Christian Education, I felt more strongly the call to the ordained ministry I had felt in the mountains. Although, through my Princeton roommate Joyce, whom I admired and who had been a candidate for the ordained ministry, I had learned that the ministry field was only cautiously open to women, I resigned my position in Indiana, packed my bags, and headed back to Princeton for further study.

Road Trip West:
Flat Land and the Grand Canyon

While I was serving as Director of Christian Education at the Indiana church, my college friend Carol, with whom I used to visit Letchworth State Park, and I decided to take a vacation together. Both Carol and I had a yearning to see California, so we made a plan to travel to Lake Tahoe and Disneyland, then stop at the Grand Canyon on the way back. We wondered how the famous canyon would compare to the one that had moved and inspired us when we were undergraduates.

On our journey west, as we entered South Dakota, the sky grew dark and foreboding. We were almost to our destination of Sioux Falls, South Dakota, but it seemed a long way off. We had never driven through territory that presented such an ominous sky. We nervously turned on the radio and learned there was a tornado warning. We were both struck with fear as we gazed at flat land with no hills nor mountains on the horizon.

"What are we supposed to do?" I asked Carol.

"I don't know," she answered distressfully. "Let's just keep heading to the motel."

After we checked into the motel and found our room, we crouched under a small table for a while. Nothing happened. We hoped the weather would improve quickly, so, with nothing but dark sky happening outside, we decided to go to bed and hope for the best.

By morning the sun was up, and we were more relaxed as we continued our journey west through more uncomfortable horizontal country.

Through this experience, I came to understand that landscape was extremely important to me. Flat land was too threatening.

On our return journey, we stopped at the Grand Canyon, as planned. By the time we reached the rim, the dry, cool air and high altitude had taken their toll on us. Accustomed as we were to the body-soaking humidity of the East, we were dehydrated. We looked at the vast desert-like chasm with tired, dry eyes and said, "What a big hole in the ground."

Little did I realize at that moment what the Grand Canyon would come to mean to me later in my life.

Jim

Princeton had changed in the five years I'd been gone. By 1974, the U.S. involvement in Viet Nam was coming to an end, and calm had descended on the seminary. Personal piety and meditation were now emphasized, and receptivity to female divinity students had grown. Male and female students were now all housed in on-campus dormitories. Concentrating in Pastoral Ministry, I began taking classes from Professors Stew Hilton and Susan Brach, learning from them how to counsel parishioners. I felt I was in the right place.

Shortly after my return, I met Jim Shannon in a worship class. We chatted before and after class, sitting next to each other most days. Little did I know how drastically my life would change after meeting this friendly Navy chaplain.

Jim and I were among the older students, and thus we'd had more life experience than many of our classmates. He'd been a chaplain for many years and was in his fourth year of seminary. The Navy was paying his tuition, so he could complete his Master of Theology degree, after which he would report to his new duty station in Norfolk, Virginia. He was nine years older than me, which was a draw for me. I also liked his mustache.

Jim and I connected for other reasons, among them, music. By the time I met Jim, he was a very accomplished jazz musician who had already had a career in music. I shared with him that I'd taken ten years of piano lessons, and later, organ lessons, and that I had substituted for organists in various churches. Jim played piano and had entertained at fairs and coffee houses throughout his college and seminary years. He had performed with various Big Bands, even after he had become a chaplain. Although I preferred classical to jazz, that didn't stop our budding romance.

Occasionally after class, Jim and I would have a cup of coffee together at the student union. One day early in our acquaintance, he told me he had a wife and four children living in Florida and that he and his wife were in the middle of a divorce. I had surmised he was either divorced or had decided his marriage was hopeless, because until then, he had never mentioned his wife, only his children.

He missed his children—Don, Jane, Tom, and Kristin, who ranged in age from twelve to seven—and spoke of them affectionately. They were all adopted, none were biological siblings, and some of them had challenging behavior issues, which his wife, Kathleen, didn't always know how to handle. Given that Jim was away so much, he was unable to parent consistently, and his family situation was not easy.

I was astounded, not so much that he was getting a divorce, as that I seemed to be developing a relationship with a man who had adopted four children. I asked myself, Should I run from this relationship or stay with it? Was it wise to be in a relationship with a man whose divorce was not final? The idea of becoming a stepmother at my age to four children I'd never met alarmed me. I was not interested in getting into the middle of such a complicated situation. On the other hand, I was very attracted to Jim.

I had had a couple of romances before. When I was at Spencer, I briefly dated Ralph, who worked at the college's radio station. He often invited me to come to the station when he was on duty as announcer. We enjoyed a secret radio station romance for several weeks, but the relationship did not go anywhere significant.

When I was at Princeton the first time, I was part of a foursome, Pete,

Dolores, and Bill being the other three. We often socialized together, and Bill and I also went on dates alone. But our relationship was more of a friendship that anything romantic and didn't feel complete to me. When I began working in Cleveland after graduation, Bill was supposed to visit me, but he never did. I knew then the relationship was over.

While my relationship with Jim had also begun as a friendship, it was slowly, surely developing into a real romance. He and I continued to talk before and after class and occasionally went on dates. While I eventually became convinced that he and his wife had no prospect of reconciliation, I still worried about the possibility that I would somehow end up caring for Jim's four children. The prospect hung like a dark cloud over our relationship.

After we had been dating for a year, I asked Jim,

"What will happen to the children if we marry?"

"They will stay with their mother. She and I have joint custody, and the agreement states they will live with her and visit me when possible."

I had visions of a crazy house full of children on weekends.

"What makes you so sure it will stay that way?" I continued.

"I suppose the unexpected could occur and one or all of the children might need to live with us, but I don't foresee that happening."

"I don't feel ready to take on four children, especially from diverse backgrounds," I said.

"I understand," he replied.

I cared about him dearly and was torn between staying with him and leaving the relationship because of my fears.

Our relationship continued to develop. I remember one special night when we went to the McCarter Theater to see a musical. It was the most enchanting night of my life. Jim came to call for me at my dormitory, and as I descended the stairs from the fourth floor in my fake fur coat and long skirt, I caught sight of him waiting for me. When I reached him, he took my hand. I cannot say what we saw at the theater, but that night I could feel our relationship moving toward marriage.

Florida Visit

While I knew I would meet Jim's children eventually, I expected to have time to prepare. But Kathleen was having difficulties with the children, and one day during the summer of 1975, she abruptly asked Jim to come for a visit. She knew Jim had been dating someone and wanted to meet me, so Jim and I boarded a plane bound for Winter Park.

We took a taxi to Kathleen's home, a Florida-style house built on a slab. I noticed the absence of a basement immediately. Kathleen met us at the door and behaved cordially. The children were courteous. I helped Kathleen prepare dinner. After we had enjoyed our meal, I spent some time with the children, talking with them about school and their various activities. Everything seemed serene and controlled. Yet I knew Kathleen had wanted Jim down there because things weren't always that way. I don't know what the two of them spoke about privately, but later, I came to believe Kathleen had begun forming a plan in which I was to become an unwilling participant.

A Wedding, a Goodbye, and Some Coddled Eggs

By the time I began my final year of study at Princeton, Jim, having completed his course work, had moved to his duty station in Norfolk. We continued to see each other on weekends when we could. He would fly to New York City and I would meet him at the train station in Princeton Junction.

My parents lifted their eyebrows over the prospect of my marrying a sailor. Sailors did not have a good reputation in my home town where, in previous years, I had seen signs reading "Dogs and sailors, keep off the lawn."

Although Jim never formally proposed to me, he did formally seek permission from my parents to marry me. When I took Jim to meet them for the first time, he dissolved their stereotypes about sailors. The fact that he came to my parents to ask permission melted their hearts.

They must have had some reservations; they were pretty conservative and concerned with propriety. They were not accustomed to any of this—sailors, divorce, or adoption. They probably wondered whether this was for real or not. Yet, given my adventurous nature, I suppose they figured such an unusual situation was par for the course for me. And the fact that Jim was a minister undoubtedly helped clinch their decision to be affirming.

They said yes.

During our preparation for marriage, we learned that Jim's ship's schedule had changed. We had been hoping to marry in the fall of 1976, but he was going to be at sea during that time, so we moved the wedding to May. Was this some kind of sign? Was our marriage going to be as wavy as the rolls of the sea? Was the fact that my birthday, second Princeton graduation, and wedding would all be packed into a few weeks also a sign? I had no way of knowing, but it did occur to me that this marriage might have a few storms in it.

Jim's divorce became final the winter before I graduated, and on May 22, 1976, we were married in my home church in Endicott. Jim was so handsome in his dress blues. I waited for him at the altar in a white wedding dress with a train. Three of my friends from college and seminary were bridesmaids; Fran was my Matron of Honor; and Jim's two older children, Jane and Don, were ushers. The ceremony, occurring within a full service of worship led by two ministers, Pastor Hertzog and Commander Rev. Dennis Kinlaw, Jim's commanding officer, was a time of great celebration. A reception followed in the church basement.

Jim and I spent our honeymoon in the Delaware River Valley, knowing we had only a short time together before we would be separated for seven months. He had orders to depart for sea duty in the Straits of Gibraltar. Too soon, his departure date arrived. As we said goodbye on the pier and I watched his ship leave, I was devastated. I felt like my world was crashing. I was in tears, wondering if I would ever see him again. Having Jim as my husband—mine alone—seemed too good to be true.

Fortunately, during the time Jim was to be on board the USS Josephus Daniels, I would have a great deal to keep me busy. I would almost immediately be entering the Medical College of Virginia in Richmond to pursue a chaplain residency in Clinical Pastoral Education.

While I hoped someday to pastor a church, I had faced the reality that the local pastorate was not yet completely open to women. Having felt I belonged in some kind of pastoral ministry since the days Pastor Hertzog had mentored me and wishing to use the skills I'd learned during my semester of CPE in Chicago, I looked forward to becoming a hospital chaplain.

However, my residency didn't start immediately, and I was lonely. As a new bride living away from base, married to a naval officer who was out to sea, I knew no one in Richmond. Shortly after I settled into our apartment, I received a phone call from Jennie Baumgardner, the wife of a chaplain with whom Jim had worked in Norfolk. Jennie and Don Baumgardner had become good friends of Jim's and consequently were now friends of mine. Jennie cheerily greeted me, then asked, "How are things going for you, Janet?"

"Okay, I guess, but it is hard to be by myself after saying goodbye to Jim. I don't know anyone here." I felt tears well up in my eyes as I embraced my loneliness and grief.

"I know," she said. "That is why I am calling—to let you know we're here if you need anything."

"Thanks, Jennie."

"Keep busy, Janet."

"I guess that won't be a problem, once the CPE group starts," I responded.

"I'm sure that's true. Keep in touch."

"Thanks, Jennie, for the call."

I hung up, grateful that Jennie, who had only recently walked into my life, cared enough to call.

A few weeks into Jim's deployment, my demanding CPE program now underway, the wife of Jim's commanding officer called.

"Hello, Janet?"

"Yes."

"This is Christie Cohn, Captain Cohn's wife."

"Oh, yes. Hi, Christie."

"How is it going for you in Richmond?"

"It's busy, but going well."

"Would you like to come down to Norfolk some weekend and spend the night with us? Maybe there is a weekend that you will be coming to the base anyway."

I was gradually getting acquainted with the people in my newly-formed Clinical Pastor Education group at the Medical College of Virginia, but I missed Jim terribly. Though my grief had diminished as I sank into the CPE process, I was still lonely in the evenings, especially as I prepared meals and sat by myself to eat. I had met Christie only briefly at a Navy function and did not know her well, but I welcomed her unexpected kindness.

"That would be great. I would like that very much. How about two weeks from now?"

"Sounds good to me."

I left work one Friday and drove the two hours to the main Naval base in Norfolk, into the officer housing area, where I easily found the Cohn house, given the detailed description Christie had given me. Christie received me with great warmth and hospitality and showed me to the beautiful, spacious guest room where I would spend the night. I was happy to be away from the rigors of the hospital training program for the weekend.

After a good night's rest, I descended the stairs and sat in a perfect-looking living room with comfortable couch and stuffed chairs with fluffy pillows.

"What do you like for breakfast?" Christie asked.

"I'm not hard to please. Cereal or anything you have is fine with me."

At that point, Christie's teenaged daughter rose to whisper something in her ear.

"I like that, too," she responded.

"It must be something special," I said.

"Yes," she responded. "We haven't had this for a while. You just sit there and read the paper and we'll be back soon."

I moved to the sun porch at Christie's suggestion and looked around at the décor and the cozy atmosphere accented with plants and pastel furniture. Soon Christie and her daughter returned with a beautiful plate of food.

"This looks wonderful. What do you call it?"

"Coddled eggs," Christie answered.

"I've never heard of them. What are they?"

"It's an English way of serving eggs," she answered. "You break the egg into a coddler and season it with cheese, green pepper, onion, mushrooms, salt and pepper. Then you screw on the top with a string through the loop of each coddler, lower them into a pan of boiling water and let them cook for 3-5 minutes."

The eggs had come out semi-soft and we ate them over toasted English Muffins as we sat on the pleasantly warm porch.

"Tell me about your training," Christie said.

I answered her questions then asked about life as the commanding officer's wife. She showed me pictures of vacations she and the children had taken while the captain was out to sea. It struck me as sad, a large aberration in a family system. She talked of activities she was involved with, such as Navy Relief, which functions as the Navy's welfare program. I was impressed by her upbeat approach to Navy life and her seeming resilience to it, despite her husband's long deployments. How does she do this? I wondered. The idea of planning vacations without Jim did not appeal to me. The image of celebrating holidays separated from Jim by miles of sea, while I collected drawers full of his letters did not enthuse me.

As she described Navy life, I wondered if it was run on a kind of caste system, with officers telling enlisted people how to live their lives. I was shocked to learn that many enlisted recruits received pay below the poverty level. Many of them held undesirable jobs, like servants. How will I get used to this? I wondered. I surmised through my conversation with Christie that it was unusual for an officer's wife to work outside the home, except as a volunteer. But I eventually hoped to pastor a church.

I was grateful to Christie for her warm hospitality as she introduced me to this strange, new life—although I realized I might have appeared strange to her.

Christie coddled me as much as the eggs we ate together.

The Crisis

JIM'S TOUR OF duty was winding down, and he proposed we spend our first married Christmas together in Palma de Majorca, Spain. How could I resist? Spending time with him in Spain would be so romantic. I packed my bags and dreamed about time with him.

I flew from Virginia Beach and was thrilled to throw my arms around him at the airport in Spain. We rented a car, a stick shift which, unfortunately, was the only car available. Jim took the wheel first. When I tried later, the result was as unproductive as when I tried driving in Uniondale as a teenager and backed over a rock, splitting the oil pan of my grandparents' car. At least I didn't actually destroy the Spanish car.

We enjoyed mild weather as we drove through hills, admiring the houses built into the hillsides and species of trees we'd never seen before. The hotel was accommodating. It appeared our room was intended for two unmarried adults, as it contained two single beds—which we promptly pushed together. Every day, our maid separated them. Every night, laughing, we slid them back together.

We had a lovely first married Christmas.

After that brief, sweet time, Jim returned to sea, and I returned to Virginia Beach.

The prospect of Jim's children coming to live with us continued to worry me. What if Kathleen were disabled to the point where the children could not continue to live with her? What if some other crisis arose that we hadn't envisioned, necessitating the children living with us? I had always been highly intuitive, and so it was with this ominous cloud shadowing my life.

As I was finishing my CPE residency in Richmond in the summer of 1977, Jim received word through his father, Harold, who lived in Minneapolis, that Kathleen had walked out on the children and had asked Harold to come down to care for them. When I heard this news from Jim, I was reminded of Dr. Seuss's *Horton Hatches the Egg*, in which a bird named Mayzie asks Horton the elephant to sit on her egg while she goes on a permanent vacation. I know people need time away from their responsibilities, but I was shocked that Kathleen had left her four children without telling Harold when or, indeed, *if* she intended to return. Kathleen appeared to be taking advantage of my having married Jim, assuming the children could now make their home with us.

I panicked. I understood that Kathleen and the children faced real challenges, with Jim being at sea so much of the time. I knew Kathleen had had serious arguments with 15-year-old Don about his behaviors—Kathleen had even called to tell me about them. But I did not understand how these difficulties were grounds for Kathleen to walk out on the children. What kind of burdens was she placing upon their shoulders and mine? I wondered.

I was scared—I did not know how to care for them. And with four needy children in the house, how could I pursue my own career? Also, at 32, my biological clock was ticking. The possibility of giving birth to my own children now seemed bleak.

I was angry at Jim. I began to think I had made a huge mistake. I should not have believed him when he said the children would never live with us permanently. With Jim moving between sea duty and shore duty, I could not count on his consistent presence. Who would help me care for these children? I knew they would eventually grow up and be out of the house, but that day was years away. I contemplated divorcing

Jim. Yet I loved him and knew I would be unhappy without him. After much prayer and contemplation, I realized it would be more detrimental to give up the marriage than to stay with it. Was God in all of this? I wondered. If so, why did this happen?

I attended my CPE group shortly after getting the news. "What's the matter?" one group member asked when he saw my distraught face. As I confided in the group and they responded, they became the Presence of God for me. One of the group members had once told us, "I often feel so helpless in light of the situations I see in the hospital. I cannot right the upset apple carts of the people I see. But I can sit on the carts with them." My group sat with me on my upturned cart, and I was grateful.

Jim arrived home on emergency leave, and we discussed the situation. "Isn't there any other place for these children to live?" I pleaded. I knew that Jim's parents, in their late 60s and having already raised six children, were not in a position to take them. Feeling desperate and trapped, I was not thinking clearly. "What about a foster home?" I asked, imagining a pair of adults experienced in caring for children. None of the possibilities I suggested were workable. Jim and Kathleen maintained joint custody of the children, so they were his responsibility as much as hers. Unlike my mother, I was not hesitant to show my anger. Jim knew I was deeply upset. He loved his children. He loved me. He knew I hadn't signed up for this. He responded to my anger by growing quiet.

Jim arranged an appointment for us to see the head chaplain about the possibility of compassionate duty, which would allow Jim to be stationed at home for the foreseeable future. We waited in the hall for Chaplain Michaelson to call us in. When he opened his office door and approached us, Jim stood and saluted. I stood also and greeted Chaplain Michaelson, stepping with both men toward the office. Chaplain Michaelson stopped and, without even glancing at me, said, "I am only going to speak with Jim." Stunned, I slowly sunk back into my chair. I felt shunned. How did this man become a chaplain, I wondered? Does he not know anything about family dynamics? As a high ranking officer, how could he be so ignorant? My eyes welled with tears. My heart overflowed with rage. I needed to be heard, to be part of the conversation. Chaplain Michaelson had probably sensed my strong feelings and decided he had better have me wait in the hallway.

When Jim reappeared, I knew by the look on his face that the conversation had not gone in our favor.

"He denied the request," Jim said somberly.

"How could he do this?!" I roared.

"He doesn't think this situation is a crisis that demands hardship duty."

"Just because he doesn't understand this is a crisis, it is—and it looms larger every minute," I retorted. "What am I supposed to do with four children who I hardly know and whose father is going back out to sea?"

The children's arrival was imminent.

Every day, I prayed, "Lord, please, please, help us!"

My Moses Prayer

When God called Moses to lead the Israelites out of Egypt, Moses told God he could not speak very well and so he was not the right person for this kind of leadership position. God did not change God's mind. God wanted Moses for the job. As I steeled myself for the children's arrival, like Moses, I tried to convince God to reconsider.

"God, you know I never liked to babysit when I was a teenager. I never knew what to do with a house full of unruly kids. A baby was okay, but I'm not getting any of those on this deal. Often I think about how I sat with a house full of misbehaving children and tried to come up with ways to corral them into bed. I loved reading stories to them, but bedtimes were a mess. God, you know that I am the youngest in my family, so I didn't have opportunities to care for younger sisters and brothers.

"Even though I've been trained to work with church youth and did so when I served as a Director of Christian Education, I didn't feel drawn to that part of ministry nor did I think I was especially adept at it. I haven't kept up with youth culture during my seminary days. Yes, I helped establish and sat in on a Parent Effectiveness Training program at the church in Indiana, and I've learned a few things about how to facilitate better communication. But I only did that for six weeks.

"God, these are my only qualifications. I am not the right person to take on the job of raising four stepchildren! I have no idea what to do with them. I feel like Moses in front of the burning bush. God, you need to look for someone else to do this job."

But God had chosen me. The children were coming.

The House

ONCE JIM'S REQUEST for compassionate leave was denied, we contacted a realtor, Mary, and began house hunting. Jim did a preliminary search with Mary, then it was my turn to go out looking with her. Because I had always lived in a house with a basement and had enjoyed the benefits of that firm foundation, I recall the day Mary showed me the house Jim and I ultimately decided on.

Mary was about fifty. Her stocky, neat appearance gave her a sense of maturity, even though she was relatively new to the career of real estate. She was the wife of a naval officer, and we talked easily together as we drove to a suburban neighborhood of Virginia Beach. The yard we stopped in front of and those around it were planted with immature trees, giving the neighborhood a new look. Mary and I entered a very pleasant-looking colonial house, built of wood and brick. The house contained four upstairs bedrooms, a family room, dining room, living room, and kitchen. The back yard was adjacent to a stream. Across the stream was a field bordered by the back of a small strip mall.

After I'd looked at the upstairs and main level, Mary and I stood in the kitchen and talked about the possibility of Jim and me buying the house. At this point, the reality of what was happening set in. My eyes welled with tears.

"I'm sorry," I said, trying to regain my composure. "It's just that all of this is happening so fast that I am having a hard time keeping it together. I know that I should be really happy, as most people are when they buy a house, but with the circumstances as they are, I am overwhelmed."

"O, Janet," Mary said. "It will be okay."

That was easy for her to say. However, as the wife of a military officer, she had at least experienced deployments, so she had some credibility. Her words offered some distant comfort. And it felt as if they were meant to address not just the purchase of a house. It was as if she was saying to me that this peculiar world of the military which I had entered contained many strange arrangements and circumstances, but people dealt with them and, somehow, they became okay.

"I hope so," I said. "It does seem like an appropriate house for the size of the family that is coming." I struggled to put my thoughts and feelings into words. I just wanted to go away to hide and scream. Instead, I said, "I don't suppose it's possible to have houses with basements here so close to the ocean?"

"No. They don't build homes with basements here because of the water level and the sandy soil." She would never know the significance of that statement.

"I'm sure that's true." I wanted to tell her how important basements were to me, but I refrained. She was already puzzled about my lack of composure. I didn't know how I could live in a house without a basement, especially since I knew stressful times were coming. Where would I go to put my world back together?

I looked down at the floor and swallowed hard before looking Mary in the face to say, "This will be fine."

What I really meant was that I would need to find some way to make it fine or at least okay. What else could I do? It was available at the time that we needed it. I liked the location. We could afford it.

As Mary and I got back in her car, I thought, people seem pretty normal here even though they don't have basements. How stupid of me to be thinking this way.

Threshold

I AM LYING in a sleeping bag on the floor of our new bedroom on a June night, the night before Jim and the children are to arrive from Florida. In a few hours, the whole place will change. My entire life will change.

I understand intellectually the biblical teaching that "all things work together for good to those who love God" (Romans 8:28), but tonight I cannot begin to imagine how that promise will unfold for me. All I can see is loss. I will lose my privacy, my morning quiet time, the chance to be alone with Jim—to feel our intimacy grow unhampered by the demands of a sudden, complex family. I will lose my career. I will lose the chance to bear and raise my own children.

I am grieving.

Jim and I have had so little time together. Now, on the eve of yet another of Jim's deployments, we're supposed to build a marriage that includes four kids with whom I'm barely acquainted. Too many questions are crowding in, my questions and the children's questions—even though I don't yet know what those will be.

Life might seem more normal after the furniture arrives, but right now nothing feels normal to me. My stomach churns. I dread the idea of filling my life with people and issues I don't want or know how to handle. I am on edge. The image I'm holding in my mind, one of slippery stones, turns to one of fierce ocean waves, drenching waves coming towards me. I am left reeling, knocked down, desperately trying to get my bearings and stand up again before the next wave breaks over me. I need a happier image. I can't come up with one. I am in a waking nightmare.

In the morning, I savor my last few hours of peace. Early in the afternoon, Jim's car pulls up in front of the house. I am in a better frame of mind, but still anxious. I watch through the large picture window of our home as the four doors of the car open and, pillows in hand, the children sleepily emerge. They hover by the car as if they don't know what to do next or whether they want to start this new adventure.

Why would they want a relationship with me? Surely, they want their own mother back. I am the third mother each of them will have, and I certainly don't expect to impress them.

How can I pick up where two mothers have left off? Neither one of them seemed to be up to the challenge. Their biological mothers placed them up for adoption, then Kathleen abandoned them. I am especially angry at Kathleen, unleashing my judgment on her, because I am the one struggling with how to help untangle this mess. Any understanding or compassion I have for her I bury under my anger, grief, and resentment. How am I supposed to proceed with this confused situation? I don't feel up to it either, but I am the only one left to do the job. For me to open the door and invite these children in is to open the door onto a scary, unknown world.

I watch Jim unload an animal carrier housing a mother cat and four kittens, the children's pets and potent symbols: a mother and four children. I do not rush out to meet my new family, but rather linger at the window.

Soon they start to shuffle through the grass and approach the house. I open the door. The children are here. My new reality has set in.

"Hello, Kristin," I say in the cheeriest voice I can find. "Hi, Don and Jane. Hi, Tom." What should I say after that?

"Hi," they answer in low, muttering tones.

"How was the trip?"

"Long," they say, almost in unison.

"It is a long way from Florida to here."

"Yeah."

"I see you brought other creatures with you. What are their names?" I ask, ushering them inside.

"The mother is Jean," Kristin answers. "We haven't named the others yet."

"I see. That will be a project for later, unless we give them away before that." I am startled that I say this so quickly.

"I like cats," I say cheerily, glad to find something happy in this strange meeting. "I had cats when I was a child. I had a mother cat that had a litter of four kittens also. I am not quite sure where we'll keep them, but let's take them into the family room for the time being." My liking for cats is dampened as I realize I now have the added responsibility of caring for five of them. I already have more than I bargained for.

I lead them to the family room. Kristin is the only blond among her darker-haired siblings. Jane is quiet. Don seems friendly. Tom tells me about the cats, and I ask if he takes care of them. "We all do," he replies, which gives me a clue that probably no one does. Suddenly I don't like cats at all.

One threshold was entered as the children passed through the door of the house, but I was aware of another more ominous threshold. We were standing together in the house, but I knew on some level, at least, that we were all far apart. The children's experiences of life were foreign to me. While my parents were not perfect, throughout my childhood, they had been stable, present, loving, and able to meet my needs. These children had experienced adoption, divorce, and abandonment; I knew nothing about such trauma. Nor did I know how they had been affected by being raised by a mother with multiple physical and emotional needs.

This new territory was foggy, and I had landed on a stone that was about to make me lose my balance and fall in the creek. Would I keep my head above water? I wasn't sure, but the only thing there was to do was to begin. That's what we did.

I led the children upstairs to show them their rooms: Kristin and Jane would be sharing, and Tom and Don would each have his own. I took them outside to show them the yard, the creek, and the field. They seemed impressed by the big field. While they explored, Jim and I shared a long hug. It was nice to know they had all made the trip safely, even though his car was on its last legs.

I don't remember the rest of that first day. But I do remember my relief when the furniture arrived the next day. Finally, we could create a semblance of order. The children helped some and ran around outside some.

Within a day or maybe two, Jim had to leave for his ship. What a downer that was! Home for the move, then gone. Now what?

DON

DON'S DUTCH HERITAGE was evident in his rosy complexion, high cheek bones, and soft brown hair. When he was up to mischief he had a short, silly laugh. He was notorious for finishing a carton of milk and placing it back into the refrigerator empty—but when I discovered him doing it, he did it less. He didn't want to be known as the person who takes the last milk in the carton.

While I could chuckle about this, other behaviors of Don's were nothing to laugh at. Kathleen had reported that Don would lose his temper and act out, and I now got to see this firsthand. Don would express his bottled-up anger often, usually by kicking in a door. You could tell by the number of busted doors in our house how often he lost control. Directives from me, such as asking him to do his chores or clean his room, would make him explode.

One day as I climbed the stairs to Don's room, I noticed one of the kittens strung up to the ceiling light fixture. This absolutely shocked me.

"Don, why is the kitten strung up in your room?" I asked, trying to sound calm.

"I don't know," he replied. He was probably being truthful about that—I doubt he was in touch with what made him do it.

"You need to untie the kitten."

"Okay," he replied and then did so.

Another day, I walked into the living room to find Don with his large King snake in the living room. "Don," I said as I went pale inside, "please take the snake back out to the garage. It really doesn't belong in the family room." I was becoming accustomed to sounding matter-of-fact in tense situations with Don, as I knew he wanted me to react with shock and surprise. "I don't want to find it slithering along on the kitchen floor," I continued. Despite my attempts at calm, I'm sure I looked startled. Having gained the satisfaction of a reaction, if only a mild one, Don soon took the snake back to its aquarium in the garage.

After doing my best to cope alone with Don's explosive anger and troubling behaviors for a few months, I enlisted the help of a therapist. Don and I met with the therapist once together; afterwards, Don would usually bicycle alone to his appointments. He didn't mind going, for which I was grateful. The fact that he kept these appointments suggested he knew he needed help, which gave me hope that he could learn to better handle his emotions and that our relationship could improve. He still had loads of anger and still vented—as evidenced by our doors—but his feelings seemed to soften after his therapy sessions. "And," I told myself, "at least he's kicking inanimate objects rather than any of us!"

As he worked through his anger, Don began to warm to me a little. Perhaps because he was older than the others, he was better able to understand his complex family situation, though I knew he was still confused about some of its dynamics. I was, too. Life had been difficult for these children, given that their mother's level of emotional resources was dubious.

I wondered how I might better relate to Don. One day, when I saw him open the front door and take his bicycle up to his room, a light went on. His bicycle was his favorite possession, and he took great pride in keeping it in shape.

"That's it!" I said to myself. "Bicycles!"

Having grown up in Dad's bicycle shop, I was able to talk comfortably with Don about bicycles.

One day, Don took a bicycle trip with a group of cyclists. When he returned home, he had a large bandage on his leg.

"What happened to you?" I asked.

"Oh. I had an accident," he said.

"What kind of accident?"

"I was riding along and I collided with another cyclist. Our bikes became intertwined at the wheel and I fell. I got this cut on my leg."

"What did you do for it?" I asked.

"I ran into the ocean, bleeding, and then someone gave me a bandage. The ocean about killed me because of the salt in the wound. "

"I'm sure the ocean helped to disinfect it some, but did you receive any other first aid?"

"No. I'll be fine."

"Let me see what it looks like," I said. The wound looked deep and ugly.

"Don, we need to go to Little Creek." This was the military clinic nearest to us. "It looks like it could easily become infected, and it needs more treatment than disinfectant and a bunch of bandages. You still have some dirt in there, and it is not going to heal correctly until you have it treated."

"No. I am not going to the clinic." He was 15—too big for me to pick up and put in the car. I could tell nothing I would say would convince him to go. I just had to wait this one out.

On Monday, Don called me at the church.

"Jan? This is Don. My leg is killing me. I need to go to the clinic."

"I'm not surprised. I'll be home shortly and we'll go to Little Creek."

At the clinic, the doctor scraped Don's wound to remove the dirt, applied medication, bandaged his leg, and gave him ointment to apply twice a day. After several days, the leg started to look better and the pain stopped. I had just experienced another incident in which I learned how to deal with Don's obstinacy. My learning curve was proceeding nicely.

During that first summer we were trying to become a family, Don's interest in bicycles sparked an invitation from my parents to come to Endicott and work as an apprentice in the bicycle shop. Mom was delighted to have a boy in the house to whom she could cater. She had always liked boys better than girls. (Fran and I knew this by how she catered to them. Mom always denied it, but we knew her true feelings.) Don worked alongside Dad and two other apprentices.

I was happy to have Don go to my parents' place because it gave me a break. I also hoped it would be the thread that helped my parents feel better about my situation. Sewing the relationship in this way would be beneficial for all of us, a family who had never experienced divorce and its ugly ramifications. We were all learning together.

Stepmother Initiation

SINCE IT WAS summer, the children were outside a lot, self-supervised. Kristin, Tom, and Don quickly made friends in the neighborhood. (Jane made friends once school started.) I didn't expect much of them besides the regular completion of their chores, which seemed enough to me at the time. But we did need to accomplish one thing together: buying school clothes.

I made the mistake of taking all of them shopping together. Never do this! While I was helping one child, the other three would take the opportunity to get up to mischief—swing on clothes racks, wander to other departments, call attention to themselves in as many ways as possible.

Assuming the youngest children would start getting antsy soonest, I began the excursion by announcing, "Tom and Kristin, we're going to look for your clothes first." Other parental pronouncements I made, in quick succession, went something like this:

"Don. You don't need to make fun of every outfit that Kristin tries on. It will be your turn soon and I'm sure you don't want the other children giggling about the clothes you try on."

"Tom, stop swinging on the clothes rack. I don't want to have to pay for anything you break. Kristin, watch your mouth. I don't want to hear any more comments from you."

"Jane, we'll go to your department next. Don't make snide remarks at Kristin. That is inappropriate. Just stop it."

Finally, I decided I'd had enough. Without buying them anything, I herded the children out of the store while issuing my final pronouncement: "I'm taking you all home because you are not taking this shopping trip seriously. Come on. Let's get back in the car." I soon learned that when I had all the children with me, them not taking me seriously was the order of the day. The children did eventually get school clothes, after I took them shopping one at a time.

In September, the children started school, Don and Jane at Greenwood Senior High, and Tom and Kristin at Plaza Elementary.

Every day, something happened that made me feel I was in charge of a home for disturbed children. Not only did Don exhibit troubling behaviors, but the other three children did, too.

Jane was very quiet, depressed, and did not want to talk much to me. She would usually do the right thing, such as her chores, but reluctantly, and only with gobs of coaxing from me. I might suggest to her at dinner time that the dishwasher needed to be unloaded so Don could reload it afterwards. She would sigh and say "okay" but then relegate it to a later time that evening, which backed up the whole process of getting the deed accomplished.

"Jane," I said. "Don't forget about the dishes." "Okay," she would say. Yet the dishes usually had dried food on them before she started them.

Tom regularly got suspended from school for such infractions as talking back to the teachers, not doing his homework, or being late. I eventually discovered that he was sneaking out at night, sometimes with Kristin, and sometimes with his friend Reggie. These nighttime excursions must have occurred after I went to bed, because I would spend evenings in the family room and would have heard them leave—at least I think I would have. Their nighttime prowling explained why Tom and Kristin were so tired in the morning.

Kristin was constantly hostile and uncooperative, as well as verbally abusive, putting me down at every opportunity that presented itself. When I would ask her to do something, she would spit things at me like: "I don't need to do that!" or "You are not my mother!" She and Jane argued constantly, which made me second guess our decision to have the two girls share a room. They argued about how the room should be decorated, where the furniture should be placed, and many other things that seemed to me shouldn't be so hard to resolve.

My early morning quiet time, when I would pray and read the Bible, disappeared. I rose with my alarm clock and made sure the children were also up. I often had to rouse them. Once up, they got their own breakfasts, choosing from the selection of cereals in the cupboard. I made sure they had their school lunch money, jackets and other outdoor gear appropriate to the weather. I might check to see if Kristin or Jane had her field trip permission slip or if Don had remembered to bring the special report he'd written. They would say goodbye to me and leave for their school busses.

After the children left, I would tidy up, then decide what to cook for supper. I might pull a chicken, some pork chops, or ground beef from the freezer to thaw. Or maybe I'd make a batch of chili, soup, or stew to reheat for them later. The children generally ate my cooking without complaint, and a few of my dishes actually became favorites, including the tuna casserole we called "tuna goop" and my lasagna. While they never officially helped cook, I did wonder one night when I saw spaghetti sauce on the kitchen ceiling.

Afternoons were usually dull, with only washing clothes, housekeeping, and grocery shopping to assuage my loneliness. While Jim had established a good order of chores for the children to follow, including changing their own sheets and towels, they needed constant reminders to do them. In any case, that still left plenty for me to do. The laundry basket by the washer and dryer was almost always stuffed with the linens, towels, and clothes which accumulated daily. I drove to the grocery store at least once a week, filling the cart to bursting with food I thought the children would eat, including gallons of milk and orange juice, cookies, and fruit, and, of course, everything I needed to make daily meals. Still, Don would look in the refrigerator and ask, "How come there's never any food in the house?"

I struggled to fit my quiet time in between my responsibilities. Though that didn't always work, I often talked with God throughout my days, especially when I was feeling distraught.

On days when Tom was suspended from school, which were frequent, I had to keep track of what he was doing and where he was. Otherwise, he might head for the shopping center to shoplift or invent some other kind of mischief. I came to realize that his suspensions likely helped out the school, but they certainly did nothing to help me, a parent who still felt like a single non-parent.

I hadn't had enough time with Jim before he left to feel married and not enough time with the children to feel like a parent. I was reminded of what one of the fellows in my CPE in Richmond had said: "Janet, you've gone overnight from being a Presbyterian nun to having a family with four children."

JANE

EACH SCHOOL DAY afternoon, I heard the front door close after Jane came home from school. I would say hi to her and she would quietly return the greeting, then ascend to her room. I did not know how to poke through the wall of indifference I felt from her. She was now 14. What a terrible age to have a family break up and not know if the break was permanent or not.

She missed the friends she'd left back in her old neighborhood. Her slow movements bespoke the grief she carried. Her passive aggressiveness made it difficult for Jim and me to know how to break through to her.

But her aggression wasn't always passive. She sometimes was outright hostile. Any type of disagreement between her and Kristin about decoration or room arrangement would start the verbal firing squad. They had little in common, and peace between those two came hard.

Sundays were big days for the family as we attended the chapel service on base at Norfolk where Jim served the main chapel. After the morning service, we often took the family to Shakey's Pizza Parlor for lunch. Movies and popcorn came with this experience and it created a lively and inviting atmosphere. Jane seemed to enjoy this time. Sunday evening included a hymn sing and an informal worship service with the sailors. The service took place in a non-religious setting with piano and guitars. I'm amazed that the children, let alone the sailors—who didn't seem like regular church-goers—attended these services. But then, the services didn't require any kind of commitment. Perhaps the informality was the key.

People interacted with Jane at these services, which evoked her dramatic self. These were good moments with her, when I thought for a time that all was getting better. I became a master at deluding myself.

Jane did allow me to parent her a little. I remember the time I asked her to stand on a stool while I worked on the hem of one of her dresses. What I wasn't thinking about is that heat rises and she was now near the ceiling. She stood there attentively for a few moments, then the rising heat overcame her, and she fainted. I had never seen anyone faint before, and I was in a mild panic. I quickly got up and helped her to her feet while steadying her. She came around quickly and seemed to be okay. I had nearly finished pinning up her hem, so we continued while she stood on the floor.

Another time, Jane ran a fever of 104 with few other symptoms. When I called the clinic to ask them what to do, they told me to put her in a bathtub with cold water and to pour it over her. I followed their directions and soon her temperature came down. The next day, she stayed home from school so I could monitor her situation. Her temperature returned to normal and she returned to school the following day. I was grateful when problems with Jane were as ordinary as this.

As I reflected on my and Jim's difficulties with Jane, I wondered how many times parents missed the opportunity to communicate with their children, to build communication from an initial bonding which, in good circumstances, began at birth. I did not have that opportunity with these children and no roads appeared available into Jane's thoughts and feelings. So often I saw parents fight about details of life with their children that really did not matter, such as what clothes to wear to school or church. These thoughts brought flashbacks to times when these types of issues aggravated me as a child—such as when I would stubbornly display my disdain for the fancy clothes my mother insisted upon, especially church clothes. How important in parenting to choose the fights carefully. How important it would be, if I ever became a biological parent, to guard and build upon that very fragile bond of communication between parent and child.

Despite the pain and scars from her previous situation and, regardless of how injurious any of that was, I could tell Jane wanted to return to her mother. I sensed a whole lake of unfinished business between them. Jane needed to go and tend to it.

Hardship and Help

The task of dealing with these children loomed large. I realized that if I were to continue to live with and help nurture them, I needed emotional support. Little by little, I began to discover I had support. It came from three sources. God was already actively helping, which I became more and more convinced of. Friends were also great supports. And, I had access to the sea, a manifestation of the Divine Presence. These sources of strength encouraged me to rise above the rigors of parenting four challenging children.

Feeling particularly upset on the days Tom was suspended, I would call Pam, the Executive Officer's wife, who lived nearby with her family, for support and ideas. Pam would discuss with me what a parent of a normal family (whatever that is) might do.

"Can you put restrictions on him or take away privileges?"

"I try, but nothing is effective with him. The next day he slips back into mischief. Nothing that I can take away from him at this point will make any difference."

"Janet, I don't know what to tell you, but I hear your pain and wish I could take it away from you."

"I know and appreciate that, Pam. It's good to have your ear."

Although her well-meaning attempts to help didn't really change anything, I was grateful for Pam's friendship. She and I and Barbara, the commanding officer's wife, often had lunch together, calling ourselves the Gourmet Lunch Bunch. While our husbands sailed around on the seas consuming the offerings of various mess halls on board ship, the three of us tasted and discussed various delicacies we ordered at French restaurants in the Tidewater area (as the Norfolk/Virginia Beach area was called). We were picky about what we ordered. Barbara was interested in cooking and often amazed me with the gourmet recipes she had in her repertoire. She hoped to open a French restaurant someday, and her variety of culinary experiences added grace and laughter to our lunches. (I, on the other hand, felt fortunate to get hamburgers on the table.) This good fellowship over fancy lunches became like going to the basement for a while, where life could be constructed the way I preferred it. It was a pleasant reprieve from the rigors of my other life. When lunch was over, I emerged from my escape and plunged into the realities of that life once again.

I also had a good friend in Marilyn, the wife of the chaplain who worked with Jim at the main Navy base. She and I would often work out together at a weight-loss company and then have lunch at the restaurant next door—where the proprietor often welcomed us as "the girls from the Olympics." We enjoyed his humor, given how un-Olympian we felt. I was also grateful for weekly talks with my parents and calls to and from my sister. I took frequent walks in the neighborhood, too, chatting with neighbors mowing their lawns or watching their children. All of these connections helped me feel less isolated.

I also discovered that the military, which was responsible for separations, included a built-in support system. This system made a huge difference to me, as I hopped from one wobbly stone to another. Tidewater had numerous organizations affiliated with the Navy, attendance at which increased exponentially when the sailors were at sea. The one I found especially helpful was the Chaplains' Wives Club, a social group which included the wives of all chaplains stationed at the many different bases in the Tidewater Area and which met monthly for potluck dinners when the ships were both in and out of port. Just coming together with women similarly bereft of husbands helped me immensely.

I also attended a women's clergy group monthly. This was not a group of Navy wives, but rather a social group of ecumenical chaplains' wives who lived in the Tidewater area. I developed a friendship with LaVerba, another chaplain's wife, whose husband worked with Jim at the main Navy chapel in Norfolk. LaVerba became a constant support for me, especially when Jim was at sea.

Another organization, the Officers' Wives Club also met regularly. I attended that a few times, but found it less helpful than the other two groups.

I was fortunate, also, to live in a city by the ocean. The sea is considered by Celtic Christians to be a "thin place," a place where one can especially perceive the Divine Presence. The sea has always been strengthening to me in my spiritual life—when I am by the sea, I feel that Presence. When time allowed, I often drove to one of the military bases that had a beach and sat by the water long enough to feel inspired. I often waded into the water, so I could better immerse myself in the Divine Presence.

There is a unifying quality to the ocean. Regardless of the sense of joy or sorrow I experience, I always know that the ocean is bigger than all of that. I am comforted by that fact, and it makes the ocean stand once again as the symbol of the Almighty, ever moving and yet ever constant in being. No wonder I feel complete by the ocean.

When I went to the shore in Norfolk, next door to Virginia Beach, I found it bittersweet to watch Navy ships leaving from and returning to port, as sailors began or ended their sea duty. A deck lined with officers in white dress uniforms on a ship slowly starting out to sea presented a kind of surreal beauty. The ship's whistle made a mournful sound as the ships left the pier and moved out, while hands raised above tear-stained cheeks waved goodbye to the ship and its crew as they left for months on end. There by the sea, I could imagine being connected to Jim through the water that both brought us together and divided us.

I always made sure to be home by 3:30, when the children started arriving home from school. They would drop their books and dash outside, sometimes stopping in the kitchen to rustle up some grab-and-go food on their way out. Kristin would often run next door to see the neighbor girl who had quickly become her best friend. Sometimes one of the children would switch on the light in the family room and sit down to do homework, but usually this was one of the last tasks they accomplished each day.

In the evenings, after supper, I missed Jim the most. Once the children had completed their chores and homework and had finally—after resisting—gone to bed, I would read his letters over and over. I would then get ready for bed myself, relieved to have made it through another day. Once I discovered that Tom and Kristin were sneaking out, however, I found it hard to sleep peacefully.

On weekends, remembering how I liked the big breakfasts of my childhood, I would cook eggs, pancakes, bacon, and hash-browned potatoes, but I soon learned the children would not easily wake up to enjoy my morning cooking. When I woke them to come and eat, they descended the stairs slowly, as if I had just placed a huge burden on them.

I knew that during the seven months Jim was due to be at sea, I had to find a way to occupy myself that didn't revolve around the children. I decided to make use of my teaching degree from Spencer by placing my name on a list to be a substitute teacher. I quickly discovered that a classroom in 1977 was a far different place than any classroom I'd been in when I was growing up. While my classmates and I had enjoyed taking advantage of a substitute teacher—and I expected this would happen to me, too—we had been well-behaved compared to the junior high students I encountered. I felt I was trying to survive in a jungle (even though I'd never spent time in one). I am not sure the students learned much about Social Studies or math or English from me, because they were so bent on misbehaving. After several attempts, I decided that junior high classrooms reminded me too much of our tumultuous home and that life as a substitute teacher was not for me. I took my name off the list.

I needed to find something else to occupy my time and help me meet people, especially, if possible, well-adjusted ones. That is when I called the Tidewater Presbytery Executive, Bill Jenkins, and told him I was interested in a part-time call to a church, where I felt I'd be much happier.

Blind Creek

I UPDATED MY credentials and submitted them to the Presbytery Office. Several months later, I received a phone call from Bill.

"Janet, I have a situation right in your neighborhood that needs some pastoral leadership."

"What kind of situation?" I asked.

"The Blind Creek Church's pastor had to leave because of sexual misconduct with a member of the congregation. Would you consider taking the position of interim pastor?"

I was stunned. Though I knew how painful this kind of situation could be—one of the churches where I had served as Director of Christian Education had suffered from its previous pastor's sexual misconduct—I knew nothing about how to pastor a congregation that had suffered such a trauma. What was Bill thinking, calling me?

I chuckled. "Do you really think I am qualified? I've never been an interim pastor before, and I certainly haven't served a church with sexual misconduct as part of its recent history." But then, given my proneness to enter circumstances I knew nothing about, I followed up with "Tell me more."

"I think that with your experience in Clinical Pastoral Education, you are a very good candidate. You know how to listen and process what you hear."

"That's true," I said, "but I still think this is a tall order for someone who has never pastored a church before. I guess I could talk with the interim pastor committee of the Session, and see if it appears right to me."

"Great. I'll submit your name to them."

In today's world, I would not have been offered this assignment. Now, in order to become an interim pastor, a minister must undertake special training, but in the 1970's that training did not exist.

I immediately began to pray about this. Could this really be my first call as an ordained minister? After I'd met with the Session, I continued to pray and, despite all my reservations, it seemed right to me. I accepted the position.

Aware of how challenging it would be to care for my own needs, minister to the Blind Creek congregation, figure out how to deal with my new family, and attempt to remain sane, I felt a bit anxious and overwhelmed by the prospect of this assignment. With my new family, I had simply decided to begin, so that was what I decided to do with the Blind Creek congregation—begin, and see how things would go.

I proposed a half-day retreat for the Session so we could get acquainted and I could hear what these men and women had to say about the chaos at their church. They accepted the idea. At first, another minister served as moderator of the Session, but in time that position also came under my job description.

At the retreat, I allowed my naïveté and lack of experience to work for me: I did not bring a lot of assumptions to the discussion, and I listened hard. I then worked to develop an appropriate plan based on what I heard.

The church's situation, along with my own circumstances, helped me understand what it means to be vulnerable. What seemed right about my calling to this situation was that I knew I would be part of the community. Many members of the congregation were involved with the Navy in some way or were familiar with Navy life. We all knew the effects on marriages and family life of deployments, relocations, and absences. So, before I even met the congregation, that bond already existed between us. And then, after I became their minister, the congregation got to see first-hand the challenges I faced as a new stepmother.

Tom and Kristin demonstrated those challenges one Sunday morning when they accompanied me to church, where I was to lead worship. As the three of us drove to church, they were quiet—at least for our family. After they seated themselves in the middle of the nave, they looked quite composed. As I proceeded through the liturgy, they were also quiet. Then, as I began my sermon, they began to giggle. I knew they were not laughing at what I was saying, because I was not cracking jokes or being funny. I kept speaking, trying not to look at them, because I knew they wanted to throw me off if they could. Soon, one of them whispered noisily, "Stop it!" Anticipating the escalation of a fight between them, I tensed further. At this point, most of the congregation seated in that section had turned their eyes toward the mayhem taking place. I thought of my own upbringing and how my mother would have been horrified at the children's behavior.

I remembered that once, when I was in the junior choir back in my home church, Pastor Kerr became annoyed at the din we were making. He left the pulpit, walked to the junior choir loft, and scolded us: "I am tired of you children talking so much during the service. This has to stop. This is a time to be reverent and to worship. I don't want to hear any more noise from you." After that incident of public shaming, our behavior improved immensely. We never made a peep during worship again. As I observed Tom's and Kristin's behavior from the pulpit, I wondered, should I use the same technique with them? I decided I would prefer to deal with them at home, even though that might not be effective.

While in some congregations, Tom's and Kristin's behaviors would have reflected adversely upon me as the minister, at the Blind Creek Church, the congregation seemed relieved. The minister also had problems with her children! My situation helped me bond with many congregants who had problems with their children and tensions in their families. Some came to me to share experiences and to ask for advice.

As if I had anything to offer! I was struggling, too. Many of them had husbands and fathers out to sea also. Unlike the military, which often offered unviable, ineffective solutions to problems, I offered only my own experiences, questions, and uncertainties. The congregants came to understand that their minister could enter into their struggles and understand them.

I thought I should know more than I did. With all the training I had had, I still didn't feel adequate for any of the positions I was trying to manage. But in the months I was the interim pastor at Blind Creek, I found the congregation to be as open to helping me as I was to helping them. One day I was in the kitchen with Mickey, a woman from church who was married to a Navy Chief Petty Officer and had two sons about 11 and 13. I told her about the struggles I was having with the children.

"Mickey," I said, "if parenting is this difficult, I don't ever want to have children of my own."

She looked me straight in the eye and responded, "Yes, you do. You can't judge parenting by what you experience with these children. You don't understand what it means to raise a child from the beginning."

"Mickey, your children are so well-behaved and don't get into trouble. What makes it work?"

"When you have children of your own and bring them up from birth, you have an opportunity to bond with them. Don't cheat yourself out of the chance to have children with whom you can develop this important tie. And, by the way, my children have their problems, too, as all parents and children do."

She seemed very intent, as if I really would miss something if Jim and I decided not to have children. Her plump physique standing before me somehow made her words more powerful. What she said rang in my ears because it seemed authentic and was perfectly congruent with what I perceived in her family. Mickey convinced me that having children of my own was okay. I will always be grateful to her.

I felt uncomfortable having Mickey minister to me. After all, I was her minister. I was new to parenting, pastoring, being married, and the

Navy. I was feeling my way in all of these areas. But I began to understand how to use my own vulnerability to help me in ministry and to open doors for me to work with people.

In time, I came to realize that what I thought were the congregation's expectations of me were really ones I had of myself. They reflected my own insecurity and fear of failure. I began to understand that, in being open, I wasn't letting the congregation down. Instead, I was allowing them to see my humanity. Perhaps this is one way to interpret Jesus' words in Matthew 10:39: "Those who lose their life will find it and those who find their life will lose it."

The question of how to be authentic in this situation was one I kept before me for a long time, and each day I somehow figured out how to deal with it—on some days with great success and on others, with very little. I knew that the only way to be open to other people's pain was to be in touch with my own pain and to let others see it in appropriate ways. I'm sure it became obvious to the congregation that I was still figuring things out, too.

I was surprised and gratified to learn that people liked what was happening in the church. As Bill Jenkins had predicted, the skills and insights I'd gained in CPE, which I strove to apply to both my ministry and my personal life, proved very helpful. The Session and I developed a good working relationship and, after seven months, the congregation felt they were ready to start the process to call a new minister. I had reservations about this, because I thought the healing process was still wide open to them to pursue. But they were eager to proceed with their plans to hire a new minister.

In *The Wounded Healer*, theologian Henri Nouwen writes about Christ as one through whom healing came on the cross. At Blind Creek, I learned there are smaller ways to allow one's life and vulnerability to facilitate healing for others—a new discovery for me and, I sensed, one the congregation had not witnessed before. I learned how to pick up the broken pieces of others' lives and, at the same time, be honest about my own brokenness. Together, we became the Body of Christ.

On Forgiveness

I WAS EXTREMELY happy to see Jim on his December return from sea duty. However, I found it bittersweet to remember our previous Christmas in Majorca—just the two of us.

On Christmas morning, I slowly got out of bed. The night had been short. We had attended the late night Christmas Eve service at the Navy chapel, after which Jim and I had completed last-minute, post-midnight gift wrapping. I put on my robe and slippers, then descended the stairs to the family room—to join a family I did not want.

As I rounded the corner, Jim's cheery voice greeted me. "Now we are ready!" I managed a slight smile, grateful that at least Jim was on shore duty. I couldn't imagine sharing Christmas with his children but not him.

Christmas day wore on and it was okay, even though it was not the Christmas story that I would have wanted to write for myself.

As my new life as a stepmother unfolded, I battled anger and resentment daily. I was angry at Kathleen for causing this situation, Jim for allowing it, the children for their multiple demands and maddening behaviors. Anger and resentment nearly turned my aching heart cold. They reached their tentacles into many areas of my life, causing me to become caustic and sarcastic. They built cement walls around my heart and mind, too high to scale. I was imprisoned, unable to move forward except within those walls. I ruminated around in the same dis-eased sections of my heart and mind.

Yet for me, imprisonment was artificially satisfying, at least for a while. There is safety in being angry when the anger is so huge it does not allow you to imagine what other people might be feeling.

I had always been able to forgive a minor offense when feeling transgressed by another person. The exchange of "I'm sorry" and a response of "That's okay" or "You're forgiven" rolled off my lips easily. Such an exchange was simple but genuine, because the offense did not turn me completely upside down, totally reordering my inner and outer lives. However, now that a life-changing event had arrived, I attached blame to it—I blamed Kathleen; I blamed Jim; I blamed the children; I blamed myself; I blamed God.

Just as anger and resentment did, blame, too, eased its long tentacles into my life. The more blame I cast, the more I felt justified in blaming. But after a while, blame became useless. It accomplished nothing except to keep me agitated. My need to hoard it led to my own misery and discontent, more building blocks in the walls around my heart and mind. How could reconciliation and forgiveness come to a messy, torn-up heart and life like mine?

In my CPE residency I had learned about the primal scream. When no one was around, after I'd made sure all the windows were closed, I would scream as I had been taught—scream as loudly and long as I could—expressing all my rage, anger, and frustration.

Eventually, I began to see that anger and blame created choices for me. I could continue nursing them or I could take action to dispel them. I decided to let them go. I decided to heal.

My road to healing was long and hard. My complicated anger did not unravel easily. After my decision, however, it began to dissipate a little; I no longer felt it choking me. But to truly heal, I needed to forgive.

I found that one of the biggest obstacles to forgiving others lay in my inability to forgive myself. Yes, I felt angry, but I also felt terribly guilty for being angry. When I feel guilty about something, I do not feel free. I only feel obsessed with thoughts of my guilt. Perhaps, when Jesus taught His followers to say, "forgive us our debts as we forgive others their debts" (Mt. 6:9-15), He was teaching us not only that God would forgive us if we first forgive others— but that we can only know God's forgiveness if we also forgive ourselves. I realized it was impossible for me to offer forgiveness without learning to practice it on myself. I wasn't very good at this, but felt I had to try. It seemed the only way out of my distress.

As I struggled to forgive myself, I also prayed for God's forgiveness. A breakthrough came when I realized that, after I asked God to forgive me, I needed to allow God to do so. Allowing God to forgive me at this complicated point in my life meant that I could put down the burden of anger and grief and allow God's love to flow through me.

Equipped with better understanding of both my anger and the meaning of forgiveness, I began the long, painful process of forgiving Kathleen, Jim, the children, and—yes—even God, who had given me, against my will, a new family, a new life.

Dad's Death

ONE EARLY EVENING in February of 1978, I sat in Jim's and my bedroom talking on the phone with my parents, all of us exchanging our weekly updates. I occasionally glanced outside at Inky, our cat, who was enjoying the mild winter weather.

"Oh, my! The cat just fell through the ice," I said as I looked out of the window to the stream in the back yard. "He's breaking up the ice as he thrashes around. Now he's up on shore." I could hear my Dad laugh over the phone in his usual hearty manner.

A few days later, as Jim and I prepared for bed, the phone rang. It was Fran.

"Janet, something has happened to Dad," Fran said emphatically. "We think it was a massive heart attack. Mom found him dead in the bathtub." Her words hung in the air, as if they couldn't find a way into my heart and soul.

"I was just talking with him a few days ago," I said. "He sounded fine to me."

"We thought he was fine, too. Of course, you know, Dad would never go to the doctor unless he absolutely had to or someone made him."

"Oh, I know. Mom wanted him to see a doctor many times." I felt numb.

Fran continued, telling me what Mom had told her. Dad had been out on the roof of the store chopping ice for hours. Mom worried about him being gone so long. When he came home, he ate very little dinner, then said he was going to take a bath because he felt cold. He went upstairs and she didn't hear anything for a long time. When she went to check on him, she found him lying in the bathtub, unresponsive. She called 911. The paramedics came, but he had been dead for so long, they could not attempt resuscitation.

"What a terrible shock for Mom to find him. How is she?" I asked.

"She's very upset, of course. She knows how close you were to Dad, and she didn't want to tell you. I told her you needed to know."

"Yes, of course I do. I'm glad you called," I replied.

We talked about arrangements, as much as we could. My head started to swirl with the many details I needed to attend to before I left for Endicott. As I went to the grocery store to pick up a few items, I felt as if I was in a wakeful nightmare. I wanted to scream, but couldn't. There were preparations to make, and I needed to get to Endicott as soon as possible.

Dad had taught me to ride a bike. When I was in elementary school, he had decorated my bicycles for contests, which I usually won—because Dad had all the decorations in his bike shop. Dad was the adventurous one, the one I went for walks with, who took me to the nearby park or to Ross Park Zoo. Dad was the one who held me close as ocean waves washed over me. He was the one who encouraged me to consider going to college somewhere besides the Triple Cities. He was always there to cheer me on me or give me advice. How great were his gifts to me! He had watched me graduate from high school, college, and seminary; had helped me with all my moves; had walked me down the aisle on my wedding day.

My beloved father, who had told me stories about his life before I went to bed each night, was dead. He was not going to be able to tell stories to my children. What a loss to the world, to say nothing of me! I could not envision life without my father. I was devastated.

Dad had never retired. He would not have known what to do with himself if he had. He had died the day before Valentine's Day. He had given Mom her Valentine's Day card a day early. Had he not felt well that day? Fran and I asked Mom if he had complained of any symptoms. Mom said no.

Little had I known that the goodbye I'd said at the end of our last phone conversation would be our last goodbye. I was carried away by grief.

When I saw my father in his casket, I stroked his head and kissed him and told him how much I loved him. The funeral director pulled my arm away, saying, "Why don't you just look at him?" I'm sure he didn't want me to mess up his cosmetics job.

"No," I said to him angrily. "This is my father and I will do what I need to do."

Why couldn't I have known something beforehand? Dad always shared things with me. How come I was left out of this one? The irrational question kept coming back to me, but I couldn't find an answer.

People came from out of town. My uncle came from Maryland. He talked a lot, and I hated that. Money was on his lips, his money and the state of the economy. I wanted to tear his eyes out.

"I don't want to talk about this at my father's death," I told him firmly. Then I tried to ignore him as much as possible. Other people came with food and expressions of sympathy.

The soloist at the funeral sang, "Swing Low, Sweet Chariot." I cried. We all cried. The minister spoke some words of comfort, but I don't know what they were. Dad had never missed a Sunday and always supported whoever the minister was at the time. His life was a triangle of home, work, and church, all of them within about a six block walking distance from our house.

I felt abandoned and realized I was freezing, metaphorically—that I, too, had fallen through the ice.

We were unable to complete Dad's burial immediately, because the ground was covered by three feet of snow—graves could not be dug in winter in the tiny town of Uniondale, Pennsylvania, where Dad was to be buried alongside relatives from my mother's side of the family. Instead, Dad's body was placed in a mausoleum.

On a windy April day, we made the trip back to Uniondale for his burial. Pastor Banks, a Presbyterian minister from a church in Endicott, who had known my Dad, performed the committal service. He wore a top hat that blew off during the ceremony. Fran and I started to laugh. It was the perfect thing to happen because Dad would have laughed, just as he did on the phone when I'd told him that Inky had fallen through the ice. It was good to have some relief from the heaviness of going through this ordeal for the second time.

As time passed, I became more rational, realizing that, of course, Dad had to die at some point. Since he hadn't known the time of his death, he could never have told me. Once I had firmly grasped these realizations, I began to work through the anger I had at him for not telling me ahead of time he was going to die.

But I never stopped missing him.

If the Way Be Made Clear

I'VE OFTEN WANTED the way to become clear for me. Not that I have always desired to know what God wanted me to do. Why would I want to be directed down a path which I would prefer not to travel?

After the children came, I threw away the road map for my life, the one that was supposed to lead me directly to a church or chaplaincy position of my own. Mapless, I found myself in the summer of 1978 in the role of interim pastor once again, this time at Briarwood Presbyterian Church in Norfolk, Virginia. When I started the position, I did not know how long it would take this church of 120 members to be ready for a permanent pastor. I ended up staying 18 months.

Harold Struthers, a tall, lanky, gray-haired, bespectacled, distinguished-looking man in his fifties, had served as Clerk of Session at Briarwood for 25 years, far more that the six years recommended by the Book of Order of the Presbyterian Church. No one had challenged him to relinquish his position, because they felt inadequate: he brought such eloquence and expertise to the writing of the minutes. One might argue that Briarwood would have benefited from someone who brought other qualities to the position. However, the church's boundaries were already stretched by accepting a woman as their interim pastor, a first for them. Harold's mellifluous manner of writing the minutes matched the suave, traditional style the church people had adopted. I thought it would serve me and the church better if the next pastor dealt with this situation or if Harold became incapacitated, which ever came first. After all, to have an eloquent Clerk of Session writing the minutes was not a bad perk for me.

Each month, the Session met in the fellowship hall, the only space large enough in the tiny church. After the business of the meeting was concluded, Harold would read the minutes, then pause before reciting, "These actions will take place . . . . . " and we would all join him in saying "if the way be made clear."

If the way be made clear. The phrase would resonate with me long after the meeting was over, because it encompassed the central question of my life: Am I on the right path? Before my life became complicated, I thought the right way was synonymous with the course I was taking. Now that perspective had receded, and I knew little about what came next for me. My idealism eluded me. Instead of discovering a clear way, I was fortunate to figure out the next step.

In the biblical story of God providing manna in the desert for the people of Israel, God gave them only enough for the next day. And when Jesus taught His disciples to pray, He said, "Give us this day our daily bread." The story of the manna and the words of the Lord's Prayer became more meaningful for me as I improvised my role as stepmother, day by day.

Jim served as the chaplain on the main Navy base at this time. I was glad to have him home. About nine months after I took the position at Briarwood, I became pregnant. How would I manage to care for my new baby, look after my stepchildren, and continue in ministry?

However, I was thrilled to pregnant.

The church stood in a land- and water-locked community in Norfolk. The Church members were eager to reach out to the surrounding neighborhood. After considering their options, they decided to plan a pancake supper and invite the community to it. Members of the church donated food, and a company where one member worked supplied the bacon. (Hog farming composed a large industry in

Virginia Beach.) Church members brought flour, eggs, and oil to make pancakes from scratch. Others donated syrup, orange juice, and other items not supplied out of the church budget. To make attendees feel they weren't accepting "charity," we charged twenty-five cents per meal.

Hundreds of people came, and the evening flowed with good fellowship. While the church did not gain any new members because of this outreach effort, at least not right away, the congregation had learned a way to bring hospitality to the neighborhood.

Fried Chicken

The time came for another chapel potluck, a common occurrence in the Tidewater Area, especially in the chapel community. While Jim, the children, and I had come to enjoy the food and friendship these Sunday chapel events provided, my schedule didn't always make it easy for me to attend. My full-time ministry at Briarwood kept me busy all week with work, joys, and concerns, but Sundays were particularly busy and the potlucks were always scheduled for noon, just after I'd led Briarwood's 10:30 service.

The night before the potluck, I prepared fried chicken to take to the occasion. Not being from the South, I was not confident that I had learned the knack of frying chicken successfully. Usually, when I fried it, the chicken skin stuck to the bottom of the pan, and I removed naked pieces of chicken. However, this time I thought I had mastered the culinary challenge and the chicken would come out of the pan with the skin still on it. After I'd cooked the chicken, I covered it neatly with foil and placed it in the refrigerator. I felt pretty good about my efficiency in accomplishing this task. Then I got to work preparing the next day's sermon, a task to which I always devoted a great deal of time.

The next day, I felt prepared for the day both professionally and domestically. I grabbed the pan of chicken from the refrigerator and took off for Briarwood. When I arrived, I went downstairs, placed the foil-wrapped pan in the church basement refrigerator, then went upstairs to lead the service. When worship was over, I dashed back downstairs, retrieved the pan, and drove to the chapel potluck.

When I arrived at the potluck, I took in the view of the chapel lawn: tables spread with plates, bowls, and pans of food, people standing nearby chatting. I quickly spotted Jim and the children and went over to greet them. I felt good that Jim was not on sea duty and that the whole family was there and in somewhat of a happy state. It was time to relax and enjoy ourselves.

I quickly entered the chapel and went down to the basement kitchen, where other women were placing their pans in the big oven to warm or collecting their culinary contributions from the refrigerator, where they'd placed them earlier. I said hello, set my pan in the oven, and went back outside.

After I had chatted with people for a while, one of my friends approached me with a slight grin and said, "Hi, Jan. Your lasagna is delicious."

"My lasagna? I didn't bring lasagna. It must be someone else's."

"It looks like your pan. I think it has your name on it."

I felt more and more puzzled. "Let me see what you are looking at," I replied. We went to examine the pan. As we walked to the table, a sinking feeling came over me. Could I have? I wondered. No, certainly not. But there it sat. Glaringly displayed alongside the attractive array of fresh food was a black, crusty pan of half-eaten lasagna, leftover from a supper we had consumed the night before. The pans had looked identical in the refrigerator that morning as they sat side by side. Yes, in my haste, I had grabbed the wrong pan. I felt mortified. I wanted to take it away and hide it, then bring it back halfway through the meal, to make it look like the potluck participants had eaten half of it.

As I stared at the pan, another friend said, "I had some of it. It tasted really good. "

"Thank you," I said with a chagrined smile. I was too embarrassed to come up with a clever reply. How does one respond decently in a situation like this? There was only one tolerable aspect to the situation: I was better at making lasagna than I was at making fried chicken.

I wasn't sure if people were eating the lasagna to make me feel better or if they really enjoyed it. I went with the latter. I knew people were polite in this group, but probably not that polite.

When the potluck wound down, I approached the table that had contained my contribution. As I expected, the lasagna had all been eaten. I took my crusty old pan back home.

The next evening, we quietly sat down as a family for dinner and ate chicken with the skin still on it.

Navy Wife

"Hello, Donna. How are you doing?" I greeted my neighbor over the fence in our back yards.

"I'm doing quite well, thank you. How about you?"

"Good as ever. I have been visiting a lot of people lately who have emotional problems. It's nice to have a break."

"Jan, I don't know how you have time to devote to the ministry when you have four children at home."

"I like to be busy. I feel like I'm accomplishing something."

Donna shook her head. "I can't understand it, Jan. Don't the children keep you busy enough?"

"One might say they do, but part of the reason I like ministerial work is that it's a complete change from my role at home."

"What about school meetings?"

"I attend those when I am available."

"You are something else."

"Probably not as much as you think. I know several other Navy wives with children who work outside of the home."

"Really? I don't know how they do that either."

"I really like working with people. I find it fulfilling."

"I suppose."

A Navy wife pursuing her own career was unusual in Navy culture.

While a few possessed careers of enormous value to them and others, including LaVerba, who worked part-time as a nurse in one of the local hospitals, this was rare. I did not know any other women who were occupied by their own professions as much as I was.

Much more commonly, Navy wives maintained competency in domestic skills, stayed home to nurture their children, and supported their husbands' or sons' military careers. (In those days, the person deployed was always a husband or son.)

Many Navy wives volunteered in organizations such as Navy Relief, the welfare arm of the Navy. Navy Relief consisted of women, usually officers' wives, counseling enlisted men and their wives, some of whom were below the poverty level, about their budgets. I was uncomfortable with the work these women did. They seemed to impose their middle- and upper middle-class values upon the couples they counseled. This felt wrong to me. I felt the volunteers needed to hear and understand the values of the couples they were counseling rather than judge them by their own standards. Besides, I felt sympathy for those being counseled, because Jim and I had our own financial problems—debt from his previous marriage and other factors kept us on a tight budget.

Another aspect of Navy life I could not easily assimilate involved the use of calling cards. Jim handed me a box of them when we were first married, each card printed with the words "Mrs. James Shannon." My first name faded away like wilted flowers. I had come from a seminary where women were just beginning to take hold of their right to be ordained ministers. The use of calling cards did not correlate to what I experienced at seminary, nor what I felt was justice for women.

When I entered other Navy homes, if a calling card tray did not appear obvious, I never asked about it. I only noticed such a tray in the house of one of Jim's commanding officers. I left a card there, but that was the only time.

Fortunately, my Gourmet Lunch Bunch friends, as well as other friends, were supportive of my relationship to the ministry—though it seemed sometimes as if they felt jealous of me for being able to work while Jim was gone. Because LaVerba worked outside the home, too, she wasn't jealous. Part of what made us such good friends was that we both understood the other's need to pursue her own profession, to be her own person.

Joy Ride

As I continued my ministry at Briarwood, Jim left for sea duty again. Not having him around to help was hard. The days seem longer and longer as my pregnancy progressed. I was grateful he would be back in time for the birth of our baby. At least, I hoped he would.

One night, when I was about eight months pregnant, I had climbed into bed and fallen asleep after a long day. About 2:00 a.m., I was awakened by the telephone. I picked it up with a groggy "Hello?" and heard a man's voice at the other end of the line.

"Hello, Mrs. Shannon?"

"Yes."

"This is Officer Smith at the juvenile detention center. We have your son down here. We found him and his friend driving down the highway, swerving back and forth. Would you please come down and pick him up?"

My first inclination was to say, "No, just keep him there for the night. That way I will know where he is." I knew the officer did not want to hear that. I didn't even know for sure which boy I was picking up. Since Don was the one with the driver's license, I guessed it was probably him. I must have been in a daze to think that—it was too logical.

I quickly dressed and rummaged for my keys. When I got downstairs and out the door, I saw one car where there should have been two. I got into the remaining car and drove to the detention center.

When I arrived, Tom and his friend Benedict, both thirteen, sat waiting for me, heads hanging. So, the boy I was picking up was Tom. It was like the old joke about who is on first.

I was disgusted with him, but too tired to want to feel it. I just wanted to go back to bed, but I was at the juvenile detention center instead. No place to sleep here.

I signed for both boys, speaking to neither of them, and walked them to Jim's car. I dropped Benedict at his house, speaking briefly to his parents at the door. I then silently drove Tom home, crawled back in bed, and went right back to sleep, hoping the rest of the night would be quiet. When morning came, I was glad to see that Tom was still in bed. Most parents would take that for granted. I didn't.

On another day around this time, Tom, in a rage, appeared as though he would strike me. Kristin, even in the midst of all of her angst, shouted at him, "Don't you dare hit her!" I don't know if it was because I was pregnant or if some other reason prompted Kristin's passionate protectiveness, but I sensed that she meant it. Tom never did strike me.

I believe Kristin's true self shone through that day. The incident helped me understand that she probably did care for me, and Jim, too, but that caring was often shrouded by her mixed-up emotions.

While that was the only incident that made me feel my living situation could be dangerous, it was one too many.

A Strange Request

On a typical late afternoon in Virginia Beach, skies sunny, temperatures mild, I stood in the kitchen, the curtains billowing slightly in the breeze. As I started to prepare dinner, the phone rang.

"Hello," I said.
"Is this Janet Shannon?"
"Yes."
"This is Kay from Parents Anonymous."
"Parents Anonymous?"
"Yes. We were wondering if you would come and speak to our parents' group."
"You want me to speak to a parents' group?" I was puzzled.
"Yes. Someone suggested you as a speaker."
I laughed. "I don't think I'm the one you want. You must have the wrong number."
"Aren't you Reverend Janet Shannon?"
"Yes."
"Then, you're the right one. Your name was suggested to us as a good speaker for our group."
"You must be kidding."
"No, I'm not."

"Well, I don't feel qualified to speak to the group. I should probably join it instead of speaking to it."

"At least you're honest," she chuckled.

"I try. Thanks for asking anyway."

I hung up the phone wondering what I could possibly say to anyone about parenting. I hardly had any ideas as to what to do with the children I lived with. Some days later, I called to learn more about this organization. What about parenting is anonymous? I thought it might be a support group, maybe for abusive parents. Later, I discovered it was just that. I hadn't committed any child abuse yet, but there were times when I was tempted to tear into these ill-behaved children. I thought someday we might all kill each other.

It later occurred to me that someone thought it appropriate to suggest my name as a speaker. Maybe I had deceived myself. Could it be that I was managing this role better than I'd thought? Maybe. I realized that I did not see the situation the same as others did. I just did my best one day at a time. That's all I knew how to do.

A Pitcher of Cold Water

Slowly, I began to develop strategies for dealing with each of the children. About two years after the children's arrival, I stumbled across one that was perhaps a little . . . unconventional.

"Tom, it's time for you to get up for school!" I hollered, passing his room as I headed for the stairs. I heard a low groan from under his covers. After that, complete silence.

I returned to his room to try to wake him. "Tom, you're going to be late," I said, frustrated. I had grown exasperated by the frequency of this morning routine, day after day, week after week, month after month. I surprised myself by saying, "If you're not up in two minutes, I will throw cold water on you, believe me." Still no response. What little I knew about parenting suggested parents should make children responsible for their own actions. How could I make this work?

What was both wonderful and scary about Tom was that he had bushels of creative energy. As I stood at Tom's bedside, I reflected: If only Jim and I could figure out how to help him turn that energy to constructive purposes, Tom could be a great human being. He was a good-looking boy, reflecting his Italian and Greek ancestry in dark brown hair and eyes that sparkled with mischief. He was charming, the friendliest of all the children—but I had quickly learned to distrust his charisma. His affability was almost always a cover-up for some prank he was contemplating or had already pursued.

The public schools in Virginia Beach were not very creative at dealing with students' willful absences. The last thing I, the school, or the community needed was to have this delinquent twelve-year-old on the loose for the day. And Tom didn't need yet another suspension on his record. There was no way I would allow him to miss another day of school. I hesitated briefly, then, in desperation, headed downstairs to the kitchen sink.

"Here I come, Tom. I have the water." No response. Carrying a full pitcher of cold water fresh from the tap, I approached his bedside. I raised the pitcher over his head. I paused. Did I really want to make a mess in the bed? I decided that compared to the trouble of having him out of school for the day, a wet pillow and mattress were of little consequence. I tipped the pitcher, quickly dousing his head and shoulders. The response was immediate. Tom woke up, startled. And mad—but that was okay. He wangled his way out of bed as I left the room. He dressed quickly, ate a bowl of cereal, and without saying a word, ran out the door to the bus. "Yay!" I said to myself. "I got him off to school."

I never experienced any more trouble getting Tom off to school. I was both happy and amazed that this one action had caused such a drastic change in behavior. While I had accomplished only a small feat in light of the other challenges Tom presented to Jim and me, I had made our lives a little easier.

Sue's Kitchen

During the times I was pastoring the Blind Creek and Briarwood congregations, Monday mornings became the time I met with Sue, a friend who, like me, was pastoring churches in interim positions. She and I would get together over tea to look at the lectionary passages for the coming week and discuss our lives. We usually met at her house, close to both of my interim churches.

Sue and her husband owned a house in Norfolk with a homey, older-style kitchen, where they displayed a variety of teas in jars on a shelf. Sue and I usually chose between our favorites, Red Zinger and Lemon Lift. Once we'd brewed the tea, shared the events, successes, and failures of our work and personal lives during the last week, and had a few laughs, we moved into our study of the lectionary passages.

Sue's kitchen was a safe place, where she and I learned from each other's strengths and weaknesses, and cautioned or encouraged one another in helpful, insightful ways. Sometime the challenges of Scripture confronted us. Nehemiah facilitating the rebuilding of the Temple seemed far away from what we knew. Yet, Nehemiah's struggle offered hope and understanding of God's provision in difficult times. If the passage applied to us, it would most likely speak to other people also. The challenge was always to take the Word and let the Spirit speak through it in our congregations. The task was always humbling.

Sue had a daughter of five at the time and was interested in some of the problems of older children and how to cope with them. (I was interested in that, too!) I envied the ease with which she enjoyed her child. She listened carefully to my tales of tension and stress. Our time would end with prayer for ourselves, our families, our work, and the world.

Sue's kitchen was a basement for me—a different type of basement. There wasn't any make believe there. But as in other basements I had known, hurts, sorrows, and disappointments flowed freely.

Working It Out

It's difficult to describe how it happened, but as the days and months passed, I grew to care for the children, despite their quirky personalities and problems. It helped to realize what we had in common—none of us had chosen to be in the situation we were in.

I also began to understand that their lives before me had been in constant flux, with Jim regularly disappearing then reappearing with each deployment. In addition, they had experienced a number of moves.

I sensed the children were angry at Jim and confused about what to do with their emotions. Often they would display their hostility to him through silence. One time, though, Jim and Don had a talk out by the creek that made a difference for Don. By the end of Jim's deployment that time, I could see a change for the better in Don's attitude. He became much more willing to help out without complaining.

While I never went so far as to conclude that Kathleen had made the right decision by walking out, I began to consider that she had been desperate and couldn't conceive of any other recourse. How could I know which of us experienced more difficulty?

There were times I wondered if I was measuring up to what a stepparent was supposed to do. I had no models. While I had friends who commiserated with me, none of them were stepparents themselves. More than once, I thought of the cruel stepmother in *Cinderella*. While I hoped I was never that mean, I'm sure the children sometimes thought I was. Leslie Jamison, herself a stepmother, writes in "The Shadow of a Fairy Tale" (New York Times Magazine, April 9, 2017) that she felt she was "constantly being dissected for how fully or compassionately [she] had assumed [her] maternal role." I understand completely what she means.

I loved Jim and wanted to be with him—that never changed. But my situation often overwhelmed me. I now understand that articulating my thoughts and feelings to him more may have been helpful, but the atmosphere never seemed right for that. His ship schedule was so choppy—sometimes he'd be home for a few weeks, then gone for a few. These times were harder than when he left for longer deployments, because the family dynamics would change quickly in a short period of time.

When he first came home from a deployment, suddenly we had another person in the house we needed to relate to. And Jim's high-pressure schedule on board ship was different from mine at home. We would inhabit very different worlds while he was away then quickly need to adjust to sharing the same one.

Once when Jim was home, one of the cats was hit by a car and died. More sorrow was added to our jumbled-up lives. While I was sad, I was also relieved to have one less being to care for.

Another time Jim was home, I found Tom splayed out on the front lawn, drunk. I went inside and got Jim, who came out and knelt next to Tom. "Tom, we need to get you to the E.R. so you can get your stomach pumped." "Okay," Tom slurred, "whatever you think." I was grateful Jim was home to drive him.

I didn't want Jim to presume upon my generosity toward the children without some recognition from him. One night when we were in the car outside the house, I told him, "I need to feel more appreciation from you that I am receiving." I didn't get much response from him.

He seemed to struggle between balancing his loyalty to the military and his responsibilities toward me and the children. I hit a wall.

Only after another military chaplain intervened could Jim and I break through that wall. Jim heard my pain and was able to convey to me that he recognized it. After that, I became more able to forgive him and move on.

Leaving Briarwood

Briarwood Presbyterian Church welcomed their new permanent minister two weeks before Jim's ship returned. Just before I left the church, I wrote a poem that went something like this:

The church became wrapped in fear,
When they saw a female minister appear.
But since that time they've come to know
That love and compassion will
continue to flow.
It's been a time of change and transition,
But we're okay and in good condition.
So on to the future and what is in store.
With God's grace we go.
We ask for no more.

My time at Briarwood was grace-filled. The parishioners, hard-working people who liked to live, work, and play well together as they learned to reach out to people in their community and even to their minister, gave me a lot more than I gave them.

At this mixed-up, confusing time in my life, my call to Briarwood helped make the way clear for me in terms of my call to ministry. And, my time there strengthened the congregation, helping them to transition to a new minister.

God's Presence was felt in our midst. The way became clearer for both the church and me.

New Life

As I waited for Jim's ship, the USS Inchon, to come into port, I reflected on the big changes to come. Though leaving the position at Briarwood considerably reduced my responsibilities, I was entering my last month of pregnancy and knew I'd be shouldering lots of new ones soon. The church gave me a baby shower, as did Mickey, the friend from Blind Creek who had convinced me to pursue biological parenthood. I had more hand-knitted baby blankets than I could ever use.

Even though the children were out of school, none of them wanted to accompany me to see Jim's ship arrive. I knew they were filled with anger, confusion, and loss. I didn't realize then that these children were probably receiving more structure and care in our household than they had experienced before. That structure and care seemed as hard for them to receive as it was for me to give.

They had experienced many stormy seas in their young lives. Now, despite the fact that their lives were still unsettled and Jim was often out to sea, they were living with a stable parent, albeit not a parent of choice. Our household—unlikely though it might seem—could well be a safe harbor for them. When a ship is tossed about at sea, the captain can sometimes bring it to a safe harbor, where it can obtain relief from tumultuous conditions. I hoped these children could understand both that I was trying my best to create a safe harbor for them and that they had a responsibility to help me keep it safe.

Standing on the pier, waiting for the men to disembark, the sun beating down on me, I felt time pass far too slowly. Fanning myself only helped a little. But, as soon as I spotted Jim, dressed in his whites, my spirits lifted. I was very eager to see him and felt quite conscious of how big I had grown since he left.

One night a couple of weeks after Jim came home, my contractions began. As they grew more and more frequent, I turned to Jim and told him I needed to go to the hospital. I was going to be a mother again, for real this time. At the hospital, I labored for 12 hours, after which my doctor suggested I have a C-section. At that point, I was ready to have the baby any way I could.

After Deborah was born, this new person in my life assuaged my worry that I'd never have children of my own. No longer was I a woman without a biological child. My view on life changed for the better. I felt more authentic.

When we brought Deborah home, the children were silent around her at first. Gradually they warmed up to her, and enjoyed making faces and playing with her.

A few months later, Jim's ship was scheduled to move to the Naval Shipyard in Philadelphia for repairs. With the children living with me and with the demands of a new baby, I was determined not deal with another separation from Jim. I decided we would ride the ship with Jim to Philadelphia and live for nine months in Navy housing in that historic city. We found homes for the mother cat and her kittens, and left the house empty. Don decided to stay in Virginia and live with friends there. With only one more year of high school left to complete, he was doing well. He and his friends planned to work to pay the rent and buy groceries. Jim and I doubted that even with their combined income, the boys could make it financially, but they were determined to try.

Jane decided to live with her mother, traveling to Atlanta, where

Kathleen had moved to be closer to relatives. Jane attended an arts high school there, pursuing her dream of becoming an actress.

That left Tom and Kristin, six-week-old Deborah, Jim, and I to embark on this adventure. On the appointed day, we approached the huge, gray ship, a small aircraft carrier that usually transported helicopters. This time it would be carrying families.

As we climbed the gangplank and I stepped over the ship's threshold, anticipating the welcome by the ship's crew, my high heeled shoes clicked away. I soon realized my mistake.

"Your state room is one level down," Jim said.

"Down?" I reply. "You mean I have to climb down that ladder in these shoes?" I don't know why this came as such a surprise to me. I had been on board ship before, but only then did I realize I was not dressed appropriately.

"How am I going to do that in these shoes?" I exclaimed.

"I don't know. You'll just have to take it easy," he replied.

I handed Deborah to Jim, picked up the bottom of my dress and slowly, carefully descended the ladder rung by rung, one foot after the other, until I finally reached the bottom. Jim, who sensibly was not wearing high heels, managed to descend the ladder while carrying Deborah

Jim escorted Kristin, Deborah, and me to our stateroom. It contained the bare essentials: a bunk bed and a sink. Deborah slept in the port-a-crib which we had brought with us. Jim and Tom occupied a room one deck above us.

After I stabilized the port-a-crib, bedded Kristin down in the upper bunk, and fed Deborah, I wearily climbed into bed, hoping I could sleep amidst the constant drone of the ship's engine. Despite my worry, I soon I drifted off to sleep, lulled by the ship's constant roar.

Sometime in the middle of the night, I felt the bed shake. Kristin was stirring and calling to me.

"Janet?"

"Yes? What's the matter, Kristin?"

"I'm going to be sick."

"Can you make it to the sink?" I asked.

"No, I don't think so," she replied. Soon I heard a splat on the floor.

"Oh, Kristin," I said, "Get up and go to the sink." This is the pits, I thought, as I climbed quietly out of bed. Deborah was still asleep, and I wanted to keep it that way. The room contained no cleaning supplies, and I was not going out of the cabin to look for them in my night clothes, so I wiped up vomit from the floor with paper towels, then cleaned the floor with soap and water.

As I finished washing the floor, Kristin climbed back into bed.

"Are you okay now, Kristin? "I asked.

"I don't know."

"Just try and relax a little."

"I'm trying. "

Deborah liked movement, so the ship's swaying kept her asleep, but I had had no knowledge of Kristin's propensity for seasickness. I'm not sure she did either. I hoped the ship's ventilation would be efficient enough to take care of the lingering smell of vomit.

Morning finally came, and I delighted in seeing the light of day.

After the rough night, I happily sought out breakfast, which quickly appeared in front of me in the mess hall. The morning's full course breakfast consisted of bacon and sausage, pancakes and eggs made to order, a variety of juices, plus plenty of hot coffee. Crisply uniformed seamen stood ready to wait on us during this entire repast. I returned to our room, gathered up our few scattered belongings and prepared to disembark. The rest of our goods were to arrive the next day on the moving van.

As we disembarked, I noticed the decommissioned ships in mothballs, looking tired and worn. I compared them to the beautiful, active ships coming and going in Norfolk, aware that the duties these ships had performed in the past were now only dimly remembered.

The large step from the ship to the pier became symbolic of the larger step our family was taking—starting a new life in a new city. I felt good knowing that, whatever difficulties we would face during this period, Jim would be there with us.

Philadelphia

As I worked in the kitchen at our townhouse, making early preparations for dinner, I gazed out the window at the Delaware River, watching the ships coming in for repair. At the end of their stay, they would once again be rendered seaworthy. Would our family have the same experience? I wondered. Would our time in Philadelphia help form the glue needed to repair our family?

I heard the front door open as Kristin arrived home from school.

"I hate that school," she said, throwing her books on the couch.

"Why do you say that?" I asked, turning toward her.

"The nuns are old and mean."

"How?"

"They really get mad if you don't have your homework done just right."

"Can you ask them for help before or after school? "

"The only chance we have is before class starts because the bus comes right after school."

"Why don't you talk with them then?"

"Because I don't want to. They're old and stupid."

"I don't think you can work this out if you don't talk to them," I reply. Kristin starts to climb the stairs to her room.

"Kristin, remember I need you to set the table."

"You can set your own table! I don't have to do what you tell me! You're not my mother!"

"I know I am not the mother you want, but she isn't here and I am, so we need to work this out."

Unfortunately, this kind of conversation between Kristin and me was not uncommon.

Before we moved, we had learned that the public schools in South Philadelphia were deplorable. Given their aggressiveness, Tom and Kristin might have been able to defend themselves when necessary in such a school, but we decided to take the advice of friends and enroll the children in the Catholic school near the base

One day shortly after we'd settled into our townhouse, we drove as a family to St. Theresa's Catholic School to enroll Tom and Kristin in seventh grade. They both sat silently in the back seat.

St. Theresa's was housed in an old brick building. The entrance led to a hallway with hardwood floors where the passages reeked with the stuffy odor of an old school. Kristin commented on the dark hallways, which didn't seem so dark to me. We followed the hall to the registrar's office.

The registrar was a helpful lay woman who was happy to enroll the children. After they were registered, she pulled out sample uniforms—white shirts and navy pants for the boys, white blouses and navy jumpers for the girls—and directed us to a nearby store where we could purchase some. Though we felt St. Theresa's was the best school for the children, we didn't think through all the ramifications of our decision. We did not take into consideration that this was a different city and the children might have difficulty making friends and fitting in.

Jim and I were delighted that discipline at the school was intact. We hoped that some of it would rub off on Tom and Kristin, especially Kristin. At home we had not found any effective way of managing her behavior, nothing to help her calm her boiling-over kettle of aggression and disrespect.

Deborah's presence aggravated the problem—she took a lot of my time and attention. Since her birth, I was not willing or able to expend as much energy to help the older children get on with their lives. Deborah's birth not only changed me but also changed the family dynamics. It helped me establish boundaries with the children I had not established before. Their behaviors also reinforced my and Jim's understanding that we needed to bond early with Deborah.

Jim and I felt helpless to recover all that had been lost in Tom's and Kristin's young lives. We did not know how to proceed beyond the walls of their defensive behavior. I was tired of trying. We sought help at a renowned family therapy clinic in Philadelphia.

"You have to be firm with these children," the therapist said as she looked mostly at me. "You are not being strict enough."

"We have tried many approaches with these children and nothing seems to make a difference. If they can't behave, I don't want to live with them. I don't want this type of environment for my baby."

"You can make the situation better," the therapist continued.

"We are doing the very best we know how and being strict hasn't helped. You may not completely understand that we did not choose this situation. The children came to us unexpectedly. I do not think they are especially committed to us being a family and, if they can't behave, I'm not committed either," I continued.

Even though the center was highly recommended to us, I was very frustrated by the therapist's approach. She was being coached by a supervisor who sat behind a mirror and said nothing during the counseling process. What type of help was he giving her? I wondered. Whatever it is, didn't help us any.

During another session, the therapist asked, "The children are not on drugs, are they?"

"No, there is no indication of that," Jim replied.

"Well then, you really don't have much of a problem."

For a moment, I wished they were on drugs, because it appeared that we would qualify for more help if they were.

After several sessions, I said to Jim, "We need to quit going to therapy. The therapist doesn't seem to get it. She doesn't understand the complexity of the problem, and I am angry and disgusted that we are constantly told we are not strict enough. Her approach is completely behavioral."

"I agree," Jim responded. We quit therapy the next day.

On October 31, 1980, my beloved Papa passed away. I felt very sad upon hearing of his death. I would miss his stories and distinctive brand of comedy. But he had died peacefully, so I felt it was okay. I was glad to be able to attend his funeral.

Despite our family difficulties, I was not disappointed that I had made the decision to come to Philadelphia. I loved being in that city. Often I walked with Deborah in the stroller while Tom and Kristin were in school. In the evening, those same streets were chockful of Mafia activities, which never affected us. I appreciated the history of the city and while we were there, we took time to visit Wyeth country, Andrew Wyeth being one of my favorite painters. Occasionally, Jim and I enjoyed dinner out at the Victor Café, where opera singers performed as we dined.

Away from my support in the Tidewater area, I needed a friend. Another chaplain's wife, Joan, pregnant with twins, lived in the townhouse directly across from us. A friendship blossomed between us. Joan didn't have to do anything remarkable to support me. Her company in itself was a joy and a solace.

Kristin continued to be unable to manage her feelings and behaviors, and we were at a loss. "What if we had Kristin live with your parents in Minnesota for a while?" I suggested to Jim. Jim's folks also had a blended family. His biological mother had died when he was twelve, and his father had married Norma. Norma brought two children from her previous marriage and, after her marriage to Jim's dad, they had five more children. They had experience rearing children and knew the difficulties of bringing families together. When Kathleen had left the children, Harold was the one who had flown to Florida to care for them until Jim could get emergency leave. "Let's ask them," Jim replied.

When his folks visited us in Philadelphia, we approached them about this arrangement and, after some consideration, they agreed to try it. Kristin was reluctantly willing to give it a try. Maybe she thought anything would be better than staying with us. I thought if this was her thought, she was probably right.

At the end of nine months, it was time for us to return to Virginia. The ship was repaired, but our family was still in shambles.

Kristin and Tom

Kristin moved to Minnesota to live with her grandparents, taking her first year in high school at a private girls' school in Minneapolis. I was relieved that this child was out of our house and hoped she could tolerate living with her grandparents.

Even though having Kristin out of our house was helpful for me, her life with her grandparents was terrible for them and for her. Harold and Norma called me several times to tell me that Kristin was climbing out of the window at night, and they feared she might be getting into drugs. Regardless of the sanctions they put upon her, she would not abide by them.

After only a couple of months, Norma called and said, "It is not working for Kristin to remain living with us."

"I understand," I said. "It is certainly not your responsibility to care for her. I appreciate all that you have done."

Kristin came back to live with us in Virginia Beach. Her attitude and her hostile approach kept most of the family at odds with her. Her speech was filled with put downs and insults. She oozed hostility, blazing a path of disdain and anger, mainly with adults and authority, though she also fought constantly with Jane and Tom. Jim struggled between his loyalty to me and his loyalty to Kristin. He wanted to respect my feelings but didn't have the tools to deal with Kristin's aggressive behavior.

Throughout this difficult time, I kept in mind the time Kristin had prevented Tom from striking me, knowing this signaled her capacity for compassion. And friendships with her peers flowed naturally, especially with the girl next door in Virginia Beach, with whom her relationship was amiable and helpful. The way I saw things: Kristin needed a lot of love, which she was afraid to accept.

Jim and I decided to have a local psychiatrist evaluate Kristin. "This child cannot live with me anymore," I said to the therapist. We talked with him for a while and after he talked with Kristin, he came back to talk to Jim and me.

"You're right," the psychiatrist said. "She should not live with you at this time. It is destructive for everyone." Wow, just like that, he had come to this conclusion. I couldn't believe it. He actually understood.

"You really mean that?" I marveled.

"Yes, this is an unworkable situation and one that is destructive to the whole family," he remarked.

He diagnosed Kristin with a type of hysteria and said he'd like to have her committed to Portsmouth Psychiatric Hospital for six weeks. "They have a section for youth," he told us, "so she'll be able to go to school there. "

Kristin entered Portsmouth Psychiatric Hospital in the winter of 1981. Jim went back to sea duty, while I met regularly with Kristin and one of Portsmouth's family therapists. At that point, I was happy to go back into therapy with her, knowing the little therapy I'd done during CPE was not enough to help me deal with her constant abusive speech. Jim joined us for the therapy whenever he was in town.

Meanwhile, Tom's problems continued to escalate. He and his accomplice, Ben, continued to raise havoc in the neighborhood. I knew he wanted and needed attention. Psychological and intelligence tests indicated there was no reason that he should do poorly in school, but his grades did not correspond to his aptitude.

One balmy day, I found Tom splayed on the front lawn drunk. I went inside to tell Jim, who came out and said, "Tom we need to get you to the emergency room so they can pump your stomach." Tom groaned as he tried to turn over but couldn't. "Okay, whatever you think," he said, slurring his words. I was grateful Jim was home on leave at this time, so he could be the one him to take him in.

Eventually, Tom and Ben committed a crime that changed everything. They torched a car in the neighborhood, completely destroying it.

Jim was out to sea the day Tom appeared in court. I remember so well the lawyer turning to Tom and saying, "Do you realize what you are putting your parents through?"

Tom hung his head and looked at the floor. "Yes," he replied.

"This is more than any parent should have to experience," the lawyer continued. I was grateful that the lawyer laid it out to him like he did. I needed another authority figure to confirm my own feelings.

While Tom awaited the court's decision, he, too, was committed to Portsmouth Psychiatric Hospital. He was there for only a few weeks, when the judge ordered him to go to reform school. I knew Tom needed to pay for his crime, but to have him sent away was painful for me. I couldn't believe myself. I hadn't initially wanted to live with him or the other children, but now that he was ordered to reform school, I felt sad. Not only had I begun to care for and love him, but I also felt that I had failed him.

It took me a while to work through my feelings of loss and failure. However, I knew Tom didn't want me to help him, at least on a conscious level. I told myself that the staff at the reform school might be better able to deal with him. Finally, I came to accept the situation, realizing it was the best option for both of us. Once again my expectations of myself had been unrealistic and I came to know it.

Our family needed as much repair as the ships in dry dock at the pier. Like them, we were broken down, but we were crossing the bridge between the old and the new. After her time at Portsmouth, Kristin opted to return to her mother.

Neither Jim nor I had been able to find a way through Kristin's defensiveness. I felt as though I had failed her, too. Even though I was gradually coming to understand I was not responsible for any of the children's deplorable behaviors, still, I felt I had failed. When Tom finished serving his time in reform school, he, too, opted to return to his mother.

We're in Michigan

In 1982, Jim, Don, Deborah, and I moved to Jim's last duty station at Selfridge Air National Guard Base near Detroit, Michigan. Soon after our move, I realized I was pregnant again.

Jane, who had difficulties after going back to live with her mother, called us and begged to be allowed to return and live with us. We agreed that she could, stipulating that if she came, she would need to enroll in school and follow through with graduation. She agreed to this and came to us soon after.

Since we lived in very cramped military housing with a carport for a garage—apparently, orders had been mixed up and the Michigan base, rather the Florida base, had received carports—space was at a premium.

My pregnancy was rocky, and eight weeks before I was due, in the winter of 1983, my water broke. I was hospitalized at a Catholic hospital in Mount Clemens, Michigan, as doctors sought to slow the delivery. Harold, named after Jim's dad, was born six weeks early. When I returned to our quarters on base, a visiting nurse came by regularly because of Harold's low birth weight. She wanted to make sure he was thriving. For the first few weeks, Hal, as we called him, needed to be fed every two hours, even if this necessitated us waking him up. I experienced post-partum depression for a while, which made the whole situation worse. This new bundle of joy was demanding!

During this time, we discovered some of Don's abilities, including his capacity to act as a short order cook for us. Don's moods were less explosive, and he became more much more congenial. He was happy to help us out where we needed it and became an important part of the family. There are two things that Don did not do at this point: go to church and keep snakes. I was very grateful for the latter. He was still interested in bicycles and kept one with him to ride wherever he could. He was somewhat bored and needed structure, and talks with Jim got him interested in joining the military.

Jane became involved with the chapel community in Mount Clements. She went to school willingly and was graduated.

One day, she surprised me by telling me she loved me. Something about the way she said it confused me. She sensed this, saying, "I love you. Do you understand what I am saying to you?"

I was starting to catch on that she had discovered she was a lesbian. Was she saying she was attracted to me? I wasn't sure I wanted to know. How did she expect me to respond? Would our relationship change now? I wasn't sure of anything.

Jane floundered after she graduated from high school. She drifted for a time, spending a lot of time reading, then enrolled in a school for the performing arts in Atlanta, where Kathleen still lived. We parted on good terms—I hugged her and gave her my blessing.

Jim retired in 1984, and a retirement ceremony was held for him on the base. We would all soon be on the move once again. Don joined the Army and left for basic training. Moving and the upheaval that goes with it had become a way of life for us. Jim, Deborah, Hal, and I spent a few months with my mother in New York State before we received a call to a church in northeastern Pennsylvania, to the town of Wilkes-Barre.

Unexpected Adventures

THE CHANGE FROM military to civilian life was fraught with difficulty. While the Navy gave orders to be followed, civilian congregations needed to foster consensus or use other voting models. Jim, our new congregation, and I all needed a period of transition to adapt—and it was not easy. Of course, Jim and I knew military life differed from civilian life, but we needed a refresher.

Our congregation expected we would operate in the same manner as the former pastor, who had been there 40 years, was a very charismatic person, and had been well appreciated by the congregation for his ways of utilizing congregational power. An interim pastor had been there for three years, but that was not long enough for this congregation to dispense with its assumptions that their next permanent pastor would operate as the previous one had. We became unintentional interim pastors, Jim full-time, and I one-quarter time, because I had young children at home.

This was the first position I had held since Deborah and Hal, now one and three, had been born. There were adjustments for me, as I needed to divide my time between church and the children. We had a wonderful woman, Dorothy, who came into our home to help with Deborah and Hal when I needed to be at the church. She was more than a babysitter—she also helped with light housework such as folding laundry, loading the dishwasher, and other small but important duties. She had no trouble finding enough to do.

Deborah and Hal loved the house in this picturesque town, because there was room for them to ride scooters through the kitchen and dining room. What was confirmed for me by this experience in Pennsylvania is that it is harder for me to work part-time than full-time, because part-time easily spills over to half- or full-time. The needs of the family and the church constituted many hours of work.

Wilkes-Barre, a provincial town, small and surrounded by coal mining, saw no protests concerning environmental issues around mining during our stay there, because consciousness had not yet been raised concerning environmental issues. We also later came to understand that the strong presence of the the Ku Klux Klan had a significant influence on the town.

Even though the Session voted in the affirmative on most of the ideas we submitted, the congregation resisted most of them. We opened a street ministry for homeless people, but members of the congregation complained that crumbs were left on the floor by the homeless and the church should no longer support this ministry. We built a learning center on the third floor of the church, but some members complained that it was too expensive to maintain. The people in the congregation exaggerated any problems that existed.

After two years, we came to an understanding with the church that we needed to leave so that other ministers could shepherd them and make decisions with them. In late summer of 1986, we packed our bags and headed to Minnesota, where Jim had grown up and gone to college and where his father and step-mother still lived. It seemed like the appropriate move to make under the circumstances, even though it left us both not knowing our future.

Minnesota Move

Despite the fact that we would be living near Harold and Norma, with whom I had a good relationship, I was not looking forward to the move to Minnesota, my sixth move since marrying Jim. Nevertheless, in the summer of 1986, I flew to Minnesota, preceding the family in order to find a house. With Don in the Army and Jane, Tom, and Kristin all in Atlanta, only Jim, Deborah, Hal, and I would be making this move.

I met with a realtor who showed me many houses in the Twin Cities and surrounding suburbs in our price range. As we drove around, I asked the realtor where the poor people lived. He told me we had just driven through that area. I was amazed. I had seen no ghettos, no dirty streets, no people lurking around as if they needed a home. Why, I wondered, was it like this?

I settled on a house in a good neighborhood in Bloomington, a second-ring suburb southwest of Minneapolis, then flew back, helped Jim finish packing, and the four of us traveled together to Minnesota.

Jim entered a doctoral program at Luther Seminary, for which he received a stipend. Through this program, he gained experience in working in prisons, such as Oak Park Heights. While he didn't finish the program, he did learn a lot about prison ministry.

I relied on my teaching degree to provide additional income, working as a substitute teacher. The wildest teaching experiences were both horrendous and hilarious. One experience had me, a social science major, attempting to teach typing to a bunch of junior high students. Another position had me running a restaurant for a home economics class.

I eventually found a position as head of Pastoral Care at Presbyterian Homes of Minnesota, in Arden Hills, a suburb of St. Paul, where I found the work quite satisfying. I worked there full-time for ten years and later worked part-time at other Presbyterian Homes' facilities in Beacon Hill and Bloomington.

Deborah started kindergarten at a private school, because we didn't know what the public schools were like in Minnesota—we assumed they would be like the public schools in Philadelphia, which we'd been warned against. Once we realized how good the local school was, we transferred her there. Hal went to a local preschool, which was held in a church and was also very good.

While times were good for us in many ways and our family finally felt relatively "normal," the hardest move I have ever made was the move to Minnesota. Part of my malaise, I'm sure, was connected to the adverse conditions under which we had left Pennsylvania. Jim and I had felt useless at the Wilkes-Barre church. People were not receptive to new ideas, and they had little confidence in us.

I also struggled with the move because, unlike neighbors everywhere else we'd ever lived, our Minnesota neighbors did not welcome us when we arrived. I couldn't help but think of the people back East who always welcomed us as their Pastor, at least when we moved to Wilkes-Barre, Pennsylvania. There the people welcomed us grandly, although part of that was because we were the new pastoral couple. I wondered about what kind of place this was to which we had moved.

One of the neighbors sold Mary Kay products, and I would have bought some from her; however, she never came to my door to sell them. We got ourselves a little Australian terrier, Fritz, and once when I was out walking him, a neighbor looked down and spoke to him but not to me! I didn't know what to make of it. Were Minnesotans shy? Extremely private? Or just unfriendly? While I've heard the term "Minnesota Nice," we experienced "Minnesota Ice."

No one approached us at church either. I learned that asking for people's names was too direct an approach, so I tried to get to know the congregation better from a distance. Rather than introducing myself to worshipers at church, I remained silent. But out of my need to get acquainted with someone, I did tell one woman that I wanted to become friendlier with her. She later told me nobody had ever said that to her before.

In Minnesota, family roots seemed all-important: family came first in a mode I had not anticipated. Biological connections seemed less important in the East, where one's family could easily be one's closest friends. No place I had lived had such an ingrown culture as Minnesota.

As I continued to struggle to understand white Minnesota culture, I came to realize Minnesotans cover up issues. Where I had lived in the past, slum areas were prevalent and obvious, especially in certain parts of town, yet that was not the case in Minnesota. I did not see any broken down homes or people on the streets. Only after I had been here for several years did I understand that many aspects of Minnesota life are quite hidden, especially the less desirable ones. One example of this is sex trafficking, which is quite prevalent in the state, especially around the Twin Cities, where we settled. It remained hidden, not talked about, and I never saw evidence of it taking place until I had lived here for several years.

I had to learn how to speak Minnesotan, as well. I came to understand that what I called a casserole was called a "hot dish" in this state. Using the word "casserole" marked me as an outsider. I learned that if I went out of the Twin Cities, even to visit a nearby town, I was going "out state," which I thought meant out of the state. The minister of a church was not called a minister but a "pastor," and people did not attend a visitation before a funeral, but a "viewing." Another new expression for me was "you betcha." My computer doesn't recognize the word "betcha." Also, I did not realize that Minnesotans did not complete some of their sentences. The first time I heard someone ask me if I wanted "to come with," I waited in vain to hear with whom, before I answered. Apparently, the "us" or "me" which was supposed to end the sentence was implied. There were times I wondered if Minnesota was really a part of the United States.

At first, I wondered if my cold reception by Minnesotans had been my fault, because I tend to be quiet. But after I realized other people had had similar experiences, I wrote an article for the local paper about my experiences and the differences I found between Minnesota and other places I'd lived. After reading the article, several people called to say how happy they were that I understood them. We set up a time to have lunch and support each other. They wanted to start a group of non-Minnesotans who had recently moved here. I did not accept the invitation, because I thought it would be more divisive than community building.

After realizing others had experienced and felt what I had, I found great courage. I decided to go with it—not that I consciously became like Minnesotans, but I found my own stride, and began to speak out about what concerned me in society, as I knew it from living in Minnesota.

When I finally began to feel somewhat settled, I began to have dizzy spells and panic attacks. Nothing seemed right, and the only diagnosis the doctors uncovered, after an MRI, was that I had a sinus infection in all my sinuses. Yes, that would be enough to make me dizzy and I was relieved that the doctors found nothing more seriously wrong in my physical being, but there seemed to be something more going on than just an infection. When the panic attacks kept coming even after my infection was resolved, I sought psychiatric help and was diagnosed with a panic disorder. I went on medication for this condition for a while which stopped the panic attacks and enabled me to work through them with the help of therapy. As biological changes stepped in to create more havoc, my world turned upside down. I felt totally out of control.

Landscape

I BEGAN TO realize that part of my difficulty lay with the landscape. Having grown up in New York State, I found Minnesota's flat land made me feel anxious and lost. Minnesotans claimed they had hills, but I could not find any hills, only some rolling countryside. How could I "lift up mine eyes unto the hills from whence cometh my help" when there were no hills (Psalm 121:1)?

I was told Minnesota was a "plains state," so I asked where the plains or prairies could be found. I learned that there are only a few prairies, in certain areas where they are set aside and preserved. Agriculture and development have led to the disappearance of the beautiful prairies. I was sad.

I thought of the Native Americans who had lived first on this land and who learned to listen to it, to hear what it wanted to become. How much understanding of nature we lost when we drove Native Americans out of Minnesota or isolated them on reservations.

I longed for mountains, and I longed for the ocean. While Minnesotans told me Lake Superior was their ocean—and I understood there are some similarities between this Great Lake and the ocean—Lake Superior could never be an ocean to me. The surf is not the same as it is in ocean cities, where I have seen it pound the shore or rocky shoals. That pounding always reminds me of God's anger. Many people prefer to cleave to the concept of God's love, but love sometimes involves anger.

I read Kathleen Norris's *Dakota* to find some comfort or solace in this strange geography where I was now living. Norris helped me eventually to recognize that flat land has its own spirituality. I began to wake up to that spirituality and to adjust to my new surroundings. I eventually felt the prairie was something I could enjoy. I began to hear its voice.

The Celtic Experience

One summer after our move to Minnesota, a friend of mine from a clergywomen's group and I attended a week-long session on Celtic spirituality at Ghost Ranch, a Presbyterian Retreat and Conference Center in New Mexico. There, Philip Newell, a creationist theologian, helped us experience the Celtic spiritual tradition. I soaked it in, feeling united with the Creator in a fresh way. As I pondered the thought that God was in everything, I slid quietly away from a hierarchical understanding of God and the world. I had never completely understood that hierarchy, in any case.

I could now begin to articulate what I had sensed while walking my grandparents' farm with Dad and stepping from stone to stone across the stream, while ocean waves crashed over me as Dad held me in his arms, while experiencing morning watch at Bible camp, while standing on mountains in my twenties and sitting beside the sea in my thirties: God was in nature.

Three years of seminary never invited me to view the world in this manner. I started to view creation differently and came to be an environmentalist.

Philip explained the difference between a pantheist and a pan-entheist. The former worships nature as God, whereas the latter worships the God who is in nature. If God is in nature, then everything is alive with the goodness of God. This understanding made my theology much more inclusive, since it showed me that every plant, animal, and mineral is part of God. I was in my forties and wondered how I went so long without realizing this truth.

Philip also talked about darkness and light. We responded to his talk by expressing our personal draws to one or the other, light or darkness. My interest in this subject piqued: I became aware that my darkest moments in life had led me to a greater understanding of light.

Sometime after the Celtic experience, I came to have a new awareness. I felt as though all my senses were alive. I called it "waking up." The author of *A Second Touch*, Keith Miller, describes the second touch of Jesus in Scripture. Perhaps I was experiencing that second touch.

Sometime later, I attended a Hymn Society Conference in Canada with Jim and was amazed that one of the keynote speakers spoke about spiritual geography. She explained that spiritual geography is about a person's natural surroundings speaking to him or her of the Divine, just as my mountain and ocean experiences had spoken to me. She quoted Belden Lane, who writes on this subject, and when I spoke with her afterward, she gave me several titles of books by Belden Lane. While I sought to understand more of this theology, several of his books found their way to my bookshelf.

I became more aware of the mess we make of creation through the ways we use and abuse our planet. Greed transforms us, causing us to turn against creation. Lane invokes this understanding of nature and pleads with people, in *Ravished by Beauty*, to sing more ardent praises to God. It makes little difference what one's scientific understanding is of the creation of the world. All of us need to understand that the huge, beautiful planet which we have inherited is something to be treasured. When I understand the ramifications of this theology, I understand the necessity of my responsibility to the planet.

Return

In the summer of 2000, I traveled back to the Uniondale church with Deborah and Hal, who had been there as toddlers and were now 20 and 17. We attended a Sunday morning service with some of the same people I'd known in my childhood, who were looking older and more fragile. These were the people who had helped to place a stepping stone for me, as I made my way toward understanding God and community.

It was many years after my grandparents had died. Since they had been elders in the church—meaning they were on the Session, the church's governing board—their names, Rennie Williams and Belle Williams, were painted on the small stained glass windows in the vestibule. After the service, Deborah used the paint I had brought along to touch up their names, while Hal rang the bell in the steeple. My grandparents had done much to keep the church going. And even more than 30 years after their deaths, they were still a part of it.

As the children and I were about to complete our visit, Hal suggested we open the outer storm-cellar door that leads to the foundation. I don't think I had ever been down there. If I had asked Dad about it, he had probably told me there was nothing to see except rock—and he would have been right. As I stood and gazed around the cold basement, I saw that, indeed, the church was built on solid rock. It was about the size of the rock in the creek in Uniondale that I had enjoyed sitting on when Dad and I would go for our rambles. The old familiar hymns "On Christ the Solid Rock I Stand" and "The Church's One Foundation" started to run through my head.

It was good to know the foundation of the church was strong. I could feel it.

A Light in the Fog

Today I am visiting my ninety-two-year-old mother, who lives in the memory care unit of the assisted-living home where I am the chaplain. I come as her daughter. I ascend the staircase to the second floor and follow the wide hallway that leads to her door. I knock and enter, calling out my cheery, "Hello, Mom."

She is sitting in her recliner, its back against the wall and her feet on the floor. She responds with a wilted, sad smile and says, "Hello." She telegraphs so many emotions through the look on her face—she tells me, without speaking, that she is not in good spirits and her conversation will probably be negative.

"Why am I still here!?" she exclaims.

"You're here because God has something left for you to do, I respond, as I sit down on the loveseat near her. This may or may not be true, at least in the way that she wants it to be true. What is left for her to do may be to die, because any type of living she does now will not be good enough for her. The dying process takes a long time for people like her, who are survivors. She has never contracted any debilitating diseases, except for the arthritis that slows her down and, now, dementia.

"I know you are very unhappy. Life just isn't the way you want it right now," I respond.

"I wish I could give piano lessons. I really miss the students," she continues. As her dementia progressed, she would have her students play the same piece over and over until they all quit. "I get lonely sometimes."

"I know you do," I say, even though I or her friends see her or talk with her nearly every day.

"We need to bring my checkbook up to date," she says.

"It's okay for now, Mom. We just did that a few days ago."

"Yes, but we are going to need to pay the rent soon."

"Yes, Mom. We will."

"We're not going to have enough money to pay it, are we?"

"Yes. We will have enough."

"Well, where are you getting all the money from?"

"From your checkbook."

During her years of keeping the books and writing the checks for our family business, Mom worried over our finances. And all of her adult life, until her dementia became apparent, she had control of her own checkbook. She resents my having control of it now.

"Who gave you permission to pay my bills?"

"You did."

"I can't remember ever turning over any power to you," she says disgustedly. She's forgotten that, years before, she granted power of attorney to Fran and me.

I seek to remain upbeat as I answer her questions over and over. Sometimes it is more than I can stand, and I have to leave because I think I am going to scream. None of my answers satisfy her. Her tone is so often angry, disgusted. Her reasoning ability is gone. She can't remember what I say, and most of it she doesn't believe anyway. She can't remember how much she forgets.

She starts to cry. "I'm lost," she says. So much of her life was spent doing—teaching piano and Sunday school, raising children, working at the family business, calling on the sick, caring for her elderly parents. Her life was composed of task after purposeful task.

She is tormented because she can't engage in the activities that she once performed so graciously. Without them, she does not know who she is. Her diminished mind does not allow her to feel any sense of accomplishment. She needs lots of attention and care to make her feel okay.

Once a week she comes to our house, bringing an apple pie she's made. This ability has not left her, nor has the inclination and aptitude to make her perfect pies. She knows exactly how long to cook the apples so they melt in your mouth. She looks for people for whom she can bake an apple pie. It helps her feel that she can still do something, but it is not enough to sustain her.

The good times become fewer and fewer, and I struggle to know what will bring her a few moments of pleasure. Usually, it is a game of Scrabble at our house or in her room. She can still form words and spell them, and she's good at it. For the duration of the game, I have her back as I once knew her, but I know it is only temporary. On the way home, or when I leave her room, her mood changes and the good time that we just had fades into the past. There is no way I can give her happiness that lasts.

Sometimes, she calls on the phone and cries through the conversation. Medication adjustments have not been successful in alleviating her misery.

"There are people here to help you with what you need," I say reassuringly.

"I wish you would shoot me," she begs.

"Mom, I know you are miserable, but we don't shoot people."

There is not much I can do for her emotional and mental state, other than to pray. Prayer is one way of turning the situation over to a Higher Power, a way to let go in one sense but stay involved in another. The moment is all there is with people suffering from dementia, and taking life moment-by-moment, the lesson I began learning with my stepchildren, is all I can do now. I take Mother's hand, we bow our heads, and I pray:

"O, God, we come to you with discontent and unease on our lips and hearts. You hear our prayer of pain. Hear the prayer of Mother as she requests that her life here on earth be over. Help her to understand that you are there for her even though she may not feel you at this moment. Through her pain and tears, grant her a sense of peace and the knowledge that she is loved. Amen."

Mother looks up at me. "You're good for someone who is depressed."

"Thank you." Her words are like sweet music. I don't need her to tell me more. I am just happy that she is able to receive something from me which, for the moment, makes her feel better. We are sharing one of those grace-filled moments that come when the way is not clear, a moment when I feel as if someone has handed me a lantern on a dark, cold, foggy night.

People say to me, "You know how to deal with it. You're trained in this." I am not trained in how to have a mother forget who she is and be angry with me for doing what I need to do for her. Understanding something about the disease may help me know what is coming next, but nothing can really prepare me for this grief, for losing the mother I once knew. I ache and bleed, like other daughters and sons in this position.

I've listened to family members of other residents at this home tell me how terrible it is to go through this. I say to them, "There are two deaths in dementia, one when you lose the person you knew because they get lost in their mind, and the other, the actual physical death." I pray with these people. They may have lost the ability to pray for themselves.

Fran comes to visit when she is in town. She puts her arm around Mother, and they sit together saying nothing, because Mother does not have the words any more. They both look peaceful.

Fran tells me, "When I look into Mother's blue-hazel eyes, it is like looking into her soul. She looks intently at me, and she is peaceful and calm. I see God in her." I am reminded of what the Jewish theologian, Martin Buber, wrote in his book, *I and Thou*. When he looked into the eyes of a cat, he felt a recognition of the other and a sense of the holy. It is the same look I see when I look into the eyes of a person whose words come haltingly or have left them, but whose soul is still alive. God is there.

Mother's Death

Up until the last few days, I had continued working at church, just going through the motions. I was not really there. I only felt present when I was with Mother. I knew I needed to be with her as much as possible.

Many days I would sit in her room and try to help with what she needed. While I appreciated the presence of the hospice staff, sometimes it seemed like an interruption. This was holy time, sacred time I wanted for myself. I was pretty sensitive about this, but I let the hospice people do their work. I knew they, too, were trying to make Mother comfortable—but the hours I was alone with her were the most precious.

How does one say goodbye to a mother who has always tried to be there for me? It seemed very strange. I couldn't imagine her dead.

Mother used to make custard to take to people who were not feeling well. I made her custard and took it to her. I was pleased to watch her eat it.

Except for periodic interruptions by hospice workers, the night before Mother died, I was alone with her. I became ready to let her die. I told her, "It is okay if you go, because Fran and I will be fine." At that point, she became more active in the dying process. That was it. Not the amount of pain killers she was given, but the fact that I had released her made the difference. I did not tell her to die. She asked me if she was dying. I asked her what she thought, and she bowed her head and closed her eyes. I did not interrupt her thoughts by presenting my own prayer. I just sat there quietly as her head was bowed. I know that at that moment, she was praying her own prayer.

When I left her, a volunteer came to sit with Mother. He seemed to understand her and told me, "She's going through a lot right now." I didn't ask him what he meant. I just let him be with her.

The next morning, I got a call with the news that Mother had slipped away during the night. It was okay. I had released her.

Fran, Again

When Fran retired from teaching, she and Dick moved to Myrtle Beach, South Carolina, where they live facing the beach. I was not aware until just recently how much she means to me. She called me to let me know about her health issues. She has calcification in all the veins in her legs, a condition which is like a time bomb. The doctor wonders if it has affected her heart, also. This explains why she has such terrible pain in her legs, especially at night. She also has fibromyalgia and back and neck issues.

Our childhood quarrels no longer matter.

The Grand Canyon Seen Anew and the Desert Appreciated

I HAD A chance to rediscover the Grand Canyon many years after my road trip with Carol, when Deborah and her husband, Rich, moved to Grand Canyon Park in Arizona.

Many times when Jim and I took a trip to see Deb's family, I would visit the Canyon. I found it enchanting. Each stone is colored differently, depending on the layer of sediment in which it's found and the way the Canyon is cut. All of the layers radiate gorgeous hues: corals, reds, yellows, blues, purples. The colors differ according to the time of day. In the morning, they are bright. The longer I stand staring, the deeper their tones grow. I feel a sense of awe.

On these trips, I didn't like having people all around me, taking pictures and *oohing* and *ahhing*. I wanted to be by myself, so I would find less populated places. When I was alone, without the clamor, I would feel overcome by the Divine Presence, as I had as a young woman when I climbed into the mountains or stood gazing across the canyon in Letchworth State Park.

On one trip, Deb, her mother-in-law, Michelle, and I were part of a group which hired a guide to take us to the bottom of the Canyon. What a trip we had! I was so focused on staying on the mule that I had a hard time concentrating on what the guide said. When we took rest stops, Michelle and I had difficulty walking because of having sat on our mules for so long. I was very happy to get to the bottom.

I was disappointed to find, however, that the cabin we were to sleep in that night had been invaded by a ringtail, relative of the raccoon. Fortunately, after we had dinner, the staff got the ringtail out.

I feel privileged to have seen and know the Canyon in so many ways.

When wilderness is a desert, as it is in Arizona, it blooms in springtime. What hope that brings during the many arid months of the year. The cacti grow white flowers, crowning themselves with beauty. I had waited a long time to see the desert in bloom. When I finally saw it, I was taken aback by the wondrous display of blooming cacti nurtured by the plants' stored water. What a natural wonder, one that fills my eyes and soul with awe.

I also felt the wind in a new way in Arizona. During one visit, we had had a busy day celebrating my grandchildren's birthdays. I found myself needing some quiet space at the end of the day, and I told Deb I was stepping outside for a few minutes. As I sat on the bench of the picnic table in the back yard, I could feel the wind gently hugging me. As my spirit came alive with the freshness of the Spirit of God, I felt strongly God renewing me.

I am intrigued by Jesus' use of wind. In John 3:8, as He talks with Nicodemus, He declares that the wind blows where it wills and we do not know from whence it comes or where it goes. Many times, on mountains and in the desert, I have felt the Spirit of God in the wind, refreshing me.

Second Honeymoon

One of the great benefits of being retired is having Jim home. After so many months and years of him being away at sea, this is such a sweet, wonderful time for us to enjoy each other. I do not understand people who complain about the person with whom they live. There are, of course, ups and downs, but at this point in life, the ups have it.

Jim and I enjoy going to movies and plays together, reading newspapers and books together. How pleasant and reassuring it is to have him near me in the evenings, as I sip my nightcap of ginger ale. If I had only known it would someday be this good, I might not have complained quite so much when Jim was out to sea and the children and I were driving each other crazy. Or, maybe I would have complained more. Who knows?

One of the great delights of our retirement is spending time in our lake cottage. (Midwesterners might call it a "cabin," but because of my eastern background, it's a "cottage" to me.) Jim and I hadn't planned to buy a cottage, but we were up in Silver Bay and decided to take a tour of places that were for sale on Lax Lake. We saw the cottage and fell in love with it. We contacted a realtor and said that we would like to see it. It didn't take long for us to decide to buy it. It had a few problems, which we repaired.

Having a lake home was something we had dreamed about, and

it became a reality. We weren't able to afford a second home when the kids were growing up and maybe that is okay, because this place is just for Jim and me now. We have decided not to share the cottage with relatives for insurance reasons.

The cottage was originally owned by a doctor and his family. While it's fairly small, it has three bedrooms. The living room leads into a hallway where the entrances to the bedrooms are. It also has a basement! The interior is decorated with what is called rosemaling. The people who owned the cottage before us told us this type of decorating was Finnish. When I looked up the word, I found that it has Norwegian influences also.

We have made the house our own by adding some of our own decorations and pictures. When Deb visited the cottage, she painted little dwarves on some of the baseboards and near one of the light switches. The dwarves hold painted signs which list the rules to follow when closing up the cottage.

The cottage is fairly close to the water and, in winter, we can look out through the trees and see people out on the lake ice fishing. I feel such a sense of peace as I gaze across the placid water and see the bluffs of Tettegouche State Forest. Houses and cottages are absent on that side of the lake to preserve the forest skyline. Birds, some different from, some the same as we have in the Twin Cities, make the trees their perches as they keep an eye out for fish or other kinds of food. What a joy to share this part of creation with them. I hear the call of the red-winged blackbird and the quiet gurgling of the mergansers. I feel alive. A sense of calm and quiet joy pervades me.

Lax Lake is not ocean-like, but it does remind me of my early experiences with the ocean, frolicking in it and playing near it. The ocean has waves, whereas I have never seen waves on Lax Lake except when a motor boat goes by. I've never dug in the sand beside the lake because there isn't any. The part of the lake shore that is swimmable is full of weeds. For a while, I tried to extract them from the water but finally gave up. We considered having a company get rid of them, but the cost is prohibitive, and there's no guarantee the weeds wouldn't return.

The cottage is about eight miles from Lake Superior. Toward the end of our four-hour drive north, as we crest the hill above Duluth, a certain excitement stirs within us. Lake Superior dominates the area from Duluth to Lax Lake. We always remark about how Lake Superior reflects what is happening on Lax Lake, especially how the color of the lake reflects so vividly in the clouds of the water.

My sense of being improves when I am beside water. I relax. As Wallace J. Nichols's writes in *Blue Mind*, humans feel a greater sense of being beside water. I am one of those humans.

Jim and I greatly enjoy the time we spend at the cottage. Certainly it is like a second honeymoon for us.

Where They Are Now

AFTER JIM'S EX-WIFE, Kathleen, passed away, the step-children began to call me "Mom." I was overjoyed that they could finally call me by the name which reflected my actions for so many years. I felt things were as they should be. And their calling me "Mom" made me feel closer to them.

My adventures as a stepmother and mother challenged me in ways I could never have imagined. All the children grew up and, for the most part, fashioned successful adult lives.

After Don left the Army, he married Clare, who came to the marriage with her daughter, Eileen. The last we knew, he was working for a company in Atlanta. He remains quite distant, and we only hear from him at Christmas. It seems that Clare is the one who sends our annual Christmas gift.

Jane never did become an actress. Instead, she started a pet care business. She was married to Janice in the summer of 2017 in Florida, where they reside. Jim and I presided at the wedding, which took place on the beach near their apartment and was followed by a beach reception. Both marrying a same-sex couple and celebrating a wedding on a beach were new experiences for Jim and me. Janice is the chef at the motel where the wedding banquet was held. We don't hear a lot from them, but they seem content. Jim and I were happy to be involved in the wedding. As a bonus, immediately preceding the wedding, I baptized Janice in the ocean. We both fell in the water. What can you expect when the surf is high?

As a young adult, Tom learned skills in food preparation. Eventually, he and his first wife, Laura, bought a deli in Key Largo, Florida, where they made cakes to send to East Coast establishments. Later, Tom moved back to Atlanta, where he learned to perform household repairs and maintenance jobs. Now, with a budding new business of his own, he hires out to do these projects. This man, who as a boy had little energy to take out the garbage or mow the lawn, is now an entrepreneur with has his own construction business. He has done well, using creativity, entrepreneurial skills, and spirit to make his way. Tom calls us a lot. He is thinking of going into management for building edifices. He and his spouse, April, do not have children, but a dog to which they are very attached. I can barely believe that he once was the child who gave me the most trouble.

Deborah lives in Arizona with her husband, Richard, and their two children, Lucy and Leo. She is a wonderful first-grade teacher and happy with her life.

Hal works for the medical device company Medtronic, lives on his own in the Twin Cities, and is doing well.

Kristin lived briefly with a friend in Blaine, a Twin Cities' suburb. She gave birth to two children, Charlie and Brenda, who live in Minneapolis—Charlie, on his own, and Brenda, with her biological father. She drove taxis and limos for a time, then moved to Oregon where, until recently, she lived with a friend.

As I was finishing this book, we received the devastating news that Kristin had died from complications of a drug overdose. She had been involved with drugs for some time—perhaps still trying to escape the pain of her early life. I think she was seeking some kind of freedom through drugs. How I wish she could have freed herself another way. I will always remember the time she prevented Tom from striking me, that moment when I glimpsed her tender side. How I wish our family's care for her could have been enough.

Epilogue

When I was a little girl, trying to know what God was all about, I stepped from my mother's Sunday school class to my father's bike shop, from the security of my basement to the freedom of my grandparents' fields, wondering, *Was God watching me? Judging me?*

From the woods that surrounded my summer Bible camp to the homes of elderly congregants, from youth group to high school, I stepped forward into what I hoped was God's will for me. In college, I slipped into the waters of doubt. Frightened, bewildered, I began to drown. I called for help. God led me to a teacher, who helped me pull myself out.

I stepped onto another college campus, into the corridors of hospitals, behind pulpits, knowing and not knowing where to go next or how trustworthy my path might prove to be. Along the way, I discovered God in trees and mountains, in the faces of the ill and dying, in the smile of my beloved.

When God gave me a big, important job to do—too big, I felt—I lost my way for a while, imprisoned by my own anger. Overwhelmed, I asked that my burdens be removed, my way be made clear, asked that I be granted discernment, skill, patience. Through the sea, the desert, the prairie, through good friends, God spoke power and comfort to me, words I could not always decipher, but still, somehow, understood. I stumbled forward, crept forward, made a path where there was none.

I have learned, after many years of stepping from stone to stone, slipping or striding, looking ahead or down at the water, that God is neither a judge to be feared nor a Santa Claus who grants wishes. The God I have come to know is the Divine Presence that infuses all creation—mountain and sea, flower and gull, cloud and child. That Presence is always within and around me, and when I let myself know that—really know it—no matter where I place my feet, I am home.

CPSIA information can be obtained
at www.ICGtesting.com
Printed in the USA
LVHW101058280323
742704LV00020B/311